T0198527

LEGACY
More than an obituary

Reverend June P. Jeffries

WESTBOW
PRESS®
A DIVISION OF THOMAS NELSON
& ZONDERVAN

WestBow Press books may be ordered through booksellers or by contacting:

WestBow Press
A Division of Thomas Nelson & Zondervan
1663 Liberty Drive
Bloomington, IN 47403
www.westbowpress.com
1 (866) 928-1240

ISBN: 978-1-9736-6847-3 (sc)
ISBN: 978-1-9736-6849-7 (hc)
ISBN: 978-1-9736-6848-0 (e)

Library of Congress Control Number: 2019908965

Print information available on the last page.

WestBow Press rev. date: 9/13/2019

I want to dedicate this book to the people who mean the world to me. First, Jesus Christ, My Lord and Savior. I know it was Him who lead me to write this legacy to my family because He wanted them to know who they are and that He has great plans for them. Then to my husband David, who supports me in loving our family and loving each other. To my children, grandchildren, and all my future generations to come, I will always love you. Last but not least, all my family inclusive of every relative by blood or by Spirit, the God given gift of family, is priceless. We are created in His image and likeness and we have been given a great gift called capacity to love and to be loved. Family don't miss out on every opportunity to love one another with words of life, it does matter.

Few come to the senior years of life and face their our own mortality without question. Aware that we are approaching the end of life, many want to go out having lived our best life. Most of us want to leave a legacy of significance and have someone speak good of us at our home-going. Pastor June Jeffries has taken it a step further. She has transcended this level of reflection on her life. In an inspirational, unselfish, passionate, reflective, and wise, work, she has written a book to her children, grandchildren, and future generations that is a testament to her life of faith in God and her ministry of love and care that will speak even beyond the grave to generations yet unborn.

Pastor Jeffries is a woman of great faith. She is, as Paul declares of himself, "not ashamed of the Gospel of Jesus Christ." As a preacher she proclaims the Gospel of Jesus Christ to persuade and inspire people to believe and come to faith in Jesus Christ. As a pastor she teaches and nurtures a congregation to grow and mature in their faith and discipleship.

This book also reveals the heart and the wisdom of a woman who is nonetheless, a mother, and grandmother, who has in view the future of offspring yet unknown and unseen. She has been inspired to write and leave a legacy that will speak long after she has transitioned life on this earth that will insure that those who carry her DNA, will not be without a knowledge of the love and power of the God that she has come to know and trust.

Rev. Dr. Joan Prentice, The Ephesus Project

Legacy is a valuable gift that Rev. June Jeffries has written for her children, grandchildren, and her future grandchildren. It is the faith walk that she shares with them in order to ensure they have the right road map to life. This gift is more precious than gold, because she reveals her soul in order to show her vulnerabilities and her victories. *Legacy* will not only bless her children and grandchildren, but all children and grandchildren. Thank you, Pastor Jeffries for pushing past your fears and doubts to share this book with the world.

Rev. Dr. Mary L. Buckley, Ed.D.,
Associate Minister, Mt. Ararat Baptist Church (Pittsburgh, PA)

Legacy Expressions

Foreword

The holy Bible is filled with promises God had made and that I believe will come to pass just as He said. One such promise is found in Deuteronomy 7:9; "Therefore know that the Lord your God, He is God, the faithful God who keeps covenant and mercy for a thousand generations with those who love Him and keep His commandments." This particular promise is significant to me for it declares that the blessings of the Lord will be bestowed upon a thousand future generations for those who have kept the commandments of the Lord. I consider myself to be one of those who have obeyed the Lord and, therefore, I believe that a thousand generations of my descendants will be shown both mercy and covenant blessings according to the Word.

Often times, when we stand on God's Word, we want to obtain the benefits without doing our part. God is a covenant God. What this means is at times, and under certain situations, His promises require that we also participate in bringing them to pass. A good example of this conditional covenant is found in the plan of salvation.

The Words states that "If we confess with our mouth the Lord Jesus and believe in our heart that God raised Him from the dead, then thou shalt be saved" (Romans 10:17). Therefore, salvation requires that we believe some things about God and Jesus and that we, if possible, speak what we believe. Even though salvation is available to every living person, only those who enter into the covenant with God will be saved.

The promises made in the Deuteronomy 7:9 require some participation and cooperation on our part. This is not a blanket blessing that, no matter what our descendants do, the holy sovereign God will bless them. At this time, my family is comprised of my three adult children and their spouses, and a total of eight grandchildren. By the time this writing is complete, I should have another grandson, making the total nine.

Family is one of God's greatest gifts given to mankind, and I am grateful for mine. I am thankful that all my children and their spouses are believers. They're not all on the same spiritual page, but they're all in the same book. That gives me the confidence that my grandchildren will also be raised to follow the word of God and will also, prayerfully, have a relationship with the Lord. The thing that concerns me, however, is how quickly generations can fall away from teaching their children the Word and regularly taking them to worship services. I have known families strong in their faith only to have a total disconnect from God one generation later. This is what I am working to avoid, if at all possible, in my family descendants and our legacy.

I want to share some of the things I've learned in this life and pray that some of my experiences will help my family members in theirs. I'm not naïve to think that my mountains and valleys will prevent them from having their own highs and lows, but my prayer is that my stories might cause them to pause and think. This is something most people would say they want for their families, but I want to do more than just hope.

My heart's desire is to gather as much love and wisdom as I can and then set it upon the foundation of the word of God and give it to my family. The thought of being able to encourage and love on children that I will no doubt never see is an awesome blessing.

Legacy—more than an obituary

I LIKE TO think of myself as a pretty good event planner. I get an idea or inspiration about something, and I'm off to the races. Day and night my mind is racing to think what else I can do, where else I can go to get the items I need to get the job done. I would describe myself as relentless in my pursuit of what I need for the perfect event. Right now, my basement is suffering with the evidence of my sometimes over-the-top shopping passions. There are way too many things stacked down there with price tags still on them while they wait to be used.

As I look back on it now, I can honestly say that I've done a pretty good job, maybe even a great job, of planning, preparing, and accomplishing those events. I pride myself in not just the plan and preparation, but also the completion of the task. To not do so would be like shopping to buy all the ingredients for a special new recipe and bringing them home, but then never making the dish.

I would also have to be honest and say these events were all about how I celebrated my life, I put all my energy into things that made life enjoyable to be celebrated—like my children's birthday parties, showers, holidays, and home remodeling. Well, what's wrong with that? I believe the Word of God has promised me that through my acceptance of Jesus Christ as my Lord and Savior, I would have life and that more abundantly (see John 10). I believe the Word!

I can't really say when it happened, but it did. I knew that I needed to write this book to and for You! You are my descendants both now and those that are yet to come. It started as a casual thought and then it grew. More and more, it became louder and louder in my spirit. I was becoming more aware of death in life. Yes, we all know we're going to die. I'm transparent and honest; I have no current health issues that make me consider my own mortality. Even though I am a Christian, knowing the promises of heaven and living eternally with Christ, death is still so unknown and therefore scary.

So, there it is, that's my confession. Now, what is God telling me to do about this truth of death that no one will escape? Oh, maybe it's to plan and prepare for death, like I do for life. I'm not afraid to die, rather, I fall more into the group that's afraid to die without having lived. So, now what? I realize quickly that the people I love are very much a part of this preparation. It's not in the pre-planning of my homegoing, but to have deliberately and intentionally left them a family legacy. I want to continue to love them even past the grave. I now feel that abundant life is the life that doesn't stop at death; rather it keeps going on and on.

So, now I begin. I must allow that same passion, energy, and determination that I used in life to help prepare me for the abundant life. Honestly, I'm quite excited about the journey. I don't know all the many places it will take me, but I'm ready to find out. I understand that to accomplish any task I must know what the goal of the task is. My task is to talk to my children and my grandchildren and my great grandchildren and on and on. I'm not sure of all the many ways I may have to go to get there, but I do have a destination. I look around the world today, and I'm deeply concerned about the moral condition the world is in. I'm not as concerned about the dissipating ozone or the extinction of whales, though these are both valid issues. My passion is for the crisis in the lives of our children.

When I was a young person, I would hear how people would quickly blame the system or certain groups of people as the reasons why they couldn't make it in life. It became every failed person's excuse for their failure. I could never fathom how some people could spend their time and energy plotting against other groups of people. To me, that just didn't make sense. Too often black men would wave it like a banner of surrender, saying, "A brother can't catch a break!"

I confess that today, I've changed my mind. Today, I'm older and wiser. I've lived long enough now to say that I've seen too much. I have seen how our culture has cultivated a group of people who are intentional concerning how their wealth and welfare depends on the oppression and suppression of others. This current culture resembles the days of the Pharaoh and the bondage of the Hebrews. Even the murder of the Hebrew baby boys was an attempt to kill the one who would come and deliver the children of Egypt from the rule of Pharaoh and slavery in Egypt.

I must admit I have always wrestled with the educational system in this country where we were taught that the pilgrims discovered America, yet the Native American Indians were already here. The Indians were dismissed as being insignificant, and in fact classified as savages so they were suppressed and ignored. I ask myself the question what would America look like today if the Indians had the guns and the Pilgrims had the bows and arrows? Also, I see systematic slavery of African Americans to work the land to make wealth for the elite at any cost. Today, way too often we see our young men shot in the back with unjust cause by officers who vowed to protect and defend, and "the wheels on the bus go around and round".

Where do I desire to go with all of this? One might ask themselves the question, what can I do against the powers that be? I was raised in a time where it was said, "You can't fight city hall". Sometimes, we choose not to engage the conflict when it looks like it's a fixed fight. I almost succumbed to the desire to do what I do, and go off into the sunset, and sit it down. Almost! Thank You, Lord, that You made me different.

We are subject in some way to the voices all around us, but there is another voice and it comes from within us. This inner voice is that of the Holy Spirit. Many times, I must quiet my own voice so that I can hear the Holy Spirit's. I trust that He knows what I need, and where I need to go, and How I am to get there. I admit that with my strong personality, I often struggle with relinquishing the reins. It gets easier to do that as spiritual maturity grows.

As I reflect, I think it might have been the movie, the *Bucket List* that made me start to think about my mortality. I thought of the things I would like to have done before I transition, and about the impact my death would have on my family. I asked myself, "Are we ever truly prepared for death?" In some ways, we are. It's important to pre-arrange our final wishes. I know death is inevitable and yet a great burden to loved ones when it comes. I think it's helpful to do as much as you can to arrange the funeral and burial and save our loved ones so many burdens.

However, now I think it's even more important to live a quality of life with as few regrets as possible, and to have loved your loved ones in ways that they know they are loved. We always think we'll have time to get things in order, but I know better now. I was referred to a book, *Falling Upward,* by Richard Rohr, in which he wrote about what I was feeling but could not find the words to express. He helped me organize my thoughts about the stage of life I was in, and what things were more important in this stage. Now, I have many things I want to accomplish, and leaving a living legacy for my children, grandchildren, and all future generations, is among the most important.

This passage accurately speaks to my deep internal desire to encourage my future generations.

> O my people, listen to me!
> Hear my instruction; soak up every word of what I am about to tell you,
> I will open my mouth in parables;
> I will speak of ancient mysteries—
> Things that we have heard about, things that we have known,
> Things which our ancestors declared to us again and again,
> We will not keep these things secret from their children;
> rather, we will tell the coming generation
> All about the praise that is due to the Eternal One.
> We will tell them all about His strength, power, and wonders.
> He gave His holy law to Jacob,

His teaching to the people of Israel,
Which He instructed our fathers
to pass down to their children
So that the coming generation would know them by
heart,
even the children who are not yet born,
So that they might one day stand up and teach them
to their children,
tell them to put their confidence and hope in God.
And never forget the wondrous things He has done.
They should obey His commandments always
And avoid following in the footsteps of their parents,
a hard-headed and rebellious generation—
A generation of uncultivated hearts,
Whose spirits were unfaithful to God (Psalm 78:1-8)
(VOICE, emphasis added)

I've never been to Africa, but I confess it's always been tucked away to do so in the back of my mind. Perhaps it's on my bucket list, and perhaps by the time this legacy is written, it will come to pass. I've had numerous people who said I would or should go there. They all say it is a life-changing experience. I think about it often, but it scares me. I'm not sure why, but I think it will affect places in me that I don't even know exist. Deep down inside I know I will go someday. One of the things I admire about Africans is how they invest in their young. For example, when living sometimes in dangerous jungles or ravines, they take the time to prepare those whom they love to survive in their environment. This is what they call the rite of passage.

The English Dictionary's definition of the *rite of passage* is "an official ceremony or informal activity that marks an important stage or occasion in a person's life, especially becoming an adult." My understanding of this African ceremonial directive came from what I saw on television. This is a critical step we have missed in this country.

When my oldest son, Delvin, went to middle school, he had many Jewish friends who celebrated their bar mitzvah, which is a form of a rite of passage. I learned from these cultural preparations that some societies intentionally prepare their young teens to transition into young adults. There is a dire need for something like this in the African American culture. We appear to have lost the sense of both urgency and obligation to prepare our young people for the real world.

My heart's desire is to begin now, and to gather as much as I possibly can, to give guidance, wisdom, and legacy to my descendants. The Lord has placed upon me the great value of two living great grandmothers, Yvonne Peeks and Helen Dennis, to give me pictures and information about my children's ancestors. What a blessing to have these amazing women help me create the big picture to begin this journey.

Every day I talk to people, or I see people on social media, celebrating their families and their accomplishments. Likewise, I see the sorrow and sadness that comes when family members transition from life to death. It's happening every day, all the time. This is something we can't control, and it seems we're never prepared for it to happen. Therefore, I'm reminded daily how important this journey is, and it keeps me engaged, and it keeps my mind always listening for "What else can I do?".

I Know You from A Distance

WHEN MY DAUGHTER, Jasmin, went back to work at Family Links after the birth of her daughter, Royal, I would babysit Royal until her dad got off from work. Jasmin would bring her around 6:30 a.m., which was much earlier than when I usually got up, so my first job was to put Royal back to sleep. I would lay her upon my chest, pat her back, and gently rock her until she fell off to sleep.

One special day as she lay upon my chest, and I felt her heart beating in rhythm with my own, I was made aware that the seed of my seed was now lying upon me, and as our hearts beat together, I realized the reality of my future generations was right now laying upon me. I was aware of the lives of children I may never see that existed now in my granddaughter. I understand how the life of the seed will lay dormant, waiting for its time to come forth as new life. Laying there, I felt a sense of connection with my future generations. This would be as close as I would ever come to many of those future generations. I felt a deep sense of life, within life, that will produce more life. I've asked the Lord to allow me to live to see five generations of my family. Of course, I think He said "Okay," but only time will tell.

I feel like even now; I'm coming to know my future generations from a distance. I was given a spiritual revelation of you that transcended time and space. When God the Creator breathed into man, His spirit and man became a living soul, and the life of that soul goes on and on. We are spirit beings, and we understand that the spirit transcends time and space, like when we pray. I've heard of how the older family mothers would pray over the womb of a pregnant family member, and even before birth they would speak words of life and purpose into their descendants. We must realize our time on earth is temporal and that we don't know when or where we may encounter life's limitations that could hinder us from fulfilling our purpose. However, when I saw you from a distance it made my heart smile as if I was with you and some of you haven't even been born yet and I knew I was on point…

Let me back up right here so you can understand the plan of God and the power of seed. The book of Genesis is the first book in the written Bible and it was recorded by Moses. It is known as the book of beginnings and it records the time of the creation of all things. It begins in this manner;

> Then God said, "Let the earth bring forth grass, the herb that yields seed, and the fruit tree that yields fruit according to its kind, whose seed is in itself, on the earth"; and it was so. And the earth brought forth grass, the herb that yields seed according to its kind, and the tree that yields fruit, whose seed is in itself according to its kind. And God saw that it was good (Genesis 1:11-12)

The creation of all things is created according to this blueprint. Everything God made either by His Word or His Hand was created with seed within itself to reproduce itself. All that He created He created pregnant with the potential to continue its kind. This is true for the single blade of grass all the way up to human beings: "Then God blessed them, and God said to them, 'Be fruitful and multiply; fill the earth and subdue it; have dominion over the fish of the sea, over the birds of the air, and over every living thing that moves on the earth'" (Genesis 1:28)

I was so excited about having the seed of my womb laying on me and the realization that my future generations are already in her womb. That's powerful! The plan of God in creation was that life would have no end and that He would dwell forever with His creation. Death only came when sin entered by way of disobedience, and the wages of sin is death. The plan of God may have gotten sidetracked, but not derailed. God has the plan for eternity, and we are all a part of the plan. We all also have a part to play in it coming to fruition.

For many, we realize that we were created for a purpose and we will live our lives on this earth endeavoring to fulfill that purpose. Others, because of free will, do not receive this truth and they will live their lives haven fallen short of their created purpose. This is a sad truth to accept, but even this shall not prevent God's plan. This is good news echoed in the gospel writings of John: "For God expressed His love for the world in this way: He gave His only Son so that whoever believes in Him will not face everlasting destruction, but will have everlasting life" (John 3:16 VOICE). This verse is fulfilled in the promise of eternal life for believers to live with Him in heaven. This is the foundation of the faith and hope we as Christians, believers in Jesus Christ, hold on to in both life and death.

I've used the word *seed* in this legacy, and I want to give you a good understanding of just how important and valuable seed is. According to *Webster's Dictionary, t*he definition of this word as a noun is *offspring or progeny,* and the synonyms are descendants, heirs, posterity, issue, or scions.

Every human being is born from a seed and is also seed-bearing. The Bible speaks of seed in the first book, which is Genesis, a word that means beginning. Everything that exists in the heavens, on the earth, and beneath the earth has its conception in Genesis. When we first read about seed it is about plants: "Then God said, 'Let the earth bring forth grass, the herb that yields seed, and the fruit tree that yields fruit according to its kind, whose seed is, on the earth'; and it was so" (Genesis 1:11). In this verse, we learn that the seed is the way life will reproduce itself and continue. Everything that God created in the world was created with the capacity to recreate itself. Life was to be eternal for everything and everybody. Then God blessed them, and God said to them, 'Be fruitful and multiply; fill the earth and subdue it; have dominion over the fish of the sea, over the birds of the air, and over every living thing that moves on the earth'" (Genesis 1:28)

Every creation of God has another life by way of the seed. There are several things I appreciate about the nature of the seed; it has potential, purpose, power, and privacy. Even though the seed is in us, we have no idea what its full potential is. No pregnant woman ever knew that the child she was carrying would be a great doctor or lawyer or even a hardened criminal. You don't know what color eyes the offspring will have or how tall or short he or she will be. There is a great mystery in a seed. No matter what, we cannot see inside ourselves and see the seed God has placed in us.

I get very excited about this. I'm looking forward to seeing all the wonderful and marvelous things that God is birthing in my seed and my seed's seed. I used to preach so much about the seed. When I was much younger, I would buy packets of vegetables seeds. I don't know why but somehow, they always ended up in the kitchen drawer. I use the tomato seed as my example, and I would say that if we leave the seed packet in the drawer, we will never be able to slice the tomato and put it on our sandwich. There are some very specific things that need to happen to the seed.

The seed must first be planted. That must happen both in literal and in spiritual applications. It's a matter of location. The seed cannot produce if it's left in a packet. Then it will need to be watered. Thank God for rain. Imagine what the earth would be like if it was left up to mankind to water the earth with a hose? So even when the seed is planted in a place that we can't see, like in the ground, the water will reach it. In my life, my tears inside and out, were both water to my seed. I remember when I had Delvin, who was born on December 22. That following New Year's Eve service, I took him with me to church. My life was in shambles. I wept so hard with him in my arms that it was like he was being baptized by my tears. I never forgot that. I wanted so bad to be a good mother for my baby boy—and I was! When I use the tomato-seed example, I point out that the water softens the outer shell of the seed. For the life within the seed to come forth, the shell must loosen its hold. Let it rain, Lord!

The next thing it needs is sunshine. The tomato needs the sun that's up in the sky; people need the Son of God. When the sun shines, it pulls the water up toward the heavens and, likewise, when we get the Son, it also pulls us heavenward. It's a beautiful thing to see when a plant breaks forth through the dirt. Even when it comes forth, we still have no idea how many big, juicy tomatoes will come from the plant. What's more, we don't know if those tomatoes will be used on sandwiches or in a pot of spaghetti; the sky is the limit.

That's why I get so excited about the potential, purpose, and plan of the seed. In one season, it can look like nothing, but hold on. God is always up to something, and just because we can't see it, doesn't mean it isn't so. Right now, you have a seed inside of you. You don't know what God is going to birth from you, but it can blow your mind! This was how God wanted it to be from the time of creation in the beginning.

One additional thing I love about the seed is the example it provides of humility. I realize a normal plant seed cannot put up any resistance to its preparation process. In a spiritual application, however, we do have free will and we must choose to submit. When we do this, it's called humility and it's admirable in the sight of God. When we as humans submit to the plan, it is a demonstration of our faith and trust in God: "Humble yourselves in the sight of the Lord, and He will lift you up" (James 4:10)

The goal of the seed is to have the life within it drawn upward and outward. This is what God will do when we humble ourselves before Him. We are not perfect people, though we are beings made into perfection, but when we fall short in our efforts, God's grace and mercy are there to pick us up. Therefore, keep trying, keep pressing, keep pushing, and keep growing.

When Adam and Eve disobeyed God's commandment in the Garden of Eden and ate the fruit they were told not to eat, sin (separation from God) came into the world, and with it came death. After that, God put His plan into action to save us from the penalty of sin and death. This plan we call the plan of salvation when Jesus, His Son and Our Savior, came to earth. Jesus became a seed for us. When He agreed to die and was buried for our sins, not His, our new life begins: "Most assuredly, I say to you, unless a grain of wheat falls into the ground and dies, it remains alone; but if it dies, it produces much grain" (John 12:24)

When we or people we love die, it can be very emotionally difficult. We miss them and it breaks our heart when they are gone from us. The good thing is that something wonderful and marvelous can still grow from their life, even after their death. It's the seed. Think of the beautiful, aromatic flowers that bloom so beautifully in their season, and then when the season and the weather changes, they die and fall to the ground. What was once so beautiful, and a delight to be around, is seemingly gone forever, but then it happens. The seed that was hidden inside of their blossoms fall to the ground, and then next spring season, new beautiful aromatic flowers bloom.

I went to a funeral some time ago for a dear sweet woman who I had known most of my life growing up. She had passed unexpectedly, and her family was so very, very sad. When many of the family members stood to give reflections, they spoke of how unselfish, loving, and family-orientated she was. They talked of ways she had shown much love to them in word and deed. It was clear that she had made a strong impression and had great influence in their lives. The character of their beloved family member was one of so many amazing assets that they could also demonstrate in their own lives, seeing that they had learned it from her example.

When I was invited to offer a few words to encourage the family, most of whom I knew, the Lord gave me an analogy to share with them about the difference between the silk flowers that were on the pulpit and the beautiful living flowers that were placed around the coffin. This is what I shared from the Lord:

When we are born, we are like fresh flowers cut out from the garden in heaven. Immediately we begin our journey towards death because our life source is in God. We only have a season of time to bloom and make an impact in the world. As we go through our time on this earth, however, we have opportunity to do two very significant things. We can leave an aroma wherever we go, and we can leave seed, which is the gift of reproduction. The aroma we give is love. Even after we are gone, it will linger in the hearts and lives of the people we've touched. And the seed will be the influence we have had on others to do the positive things that give value to life.

Unlike artificial flowers, which can appear to be equally as beautiful, but they have no fragrance, neither do they have a living seed. When we live a life without Christ, we are like these artificial flowers; our life has no real essence to leave behind. The world is full of flowers, and some look beautiful, but all you see is all you get. Others will live on and on and on because they have lived in Christ, and their fragrance of love is always in our hearts, and their seed will bloom and be made evident in our lives.

Don't wait until death comes to find out what kind of flower you are!

What's the Big Deal?

I WANT TO be very clear as to the reason I have written and recorded this legacy. I am sensitive to the Holy Spirit and the ways in which He leads me. I'm living in a time where violence; addictions; racism; political corruption; social promotion of sexual immorality; social injustice; inequality for people of color; moral and spiritual decline; lack of integrity; threat of nuclear war and family structure crisis are all the norm! The fallout from sin and its consequences are more and more manifest every day. This world is truly in a downward spiral. Despite the numerous areas of progress in technology, medicine, and science, the moral condition of men has continued to decline. At the rate we're going in 2018, I would be afraid to see how bad it will be a hundred years from now. Mankind has walked away from God's word and His commandments, and each man does what is right in his own sight:

> For the time will come when they will not endure
> sound doctrine, but according to their own desires,

because they have itching ears, they will heap up
for themselves teachers; and they will turn their ears
away from the truth, and be turned aside to fables
(2 Timothy 4:3-4)

The good news is that God already knows all this, and He's not caught off guard. He has sent His Word from the beginning to redeem lost mankind, and His word is still coming to deliver us even today!

The movie *Superman* is another source from which I gained some spiritual insight. I find this happens in all kinds of movies, and *Superman* was one such movie. The movie is a fiction story based on a character (Kea-El) from another planet who has amazing powers on earth. It starts with his parents, Joe-El and Lara -El, on the planet Krypton. They were aware that their planet was being destroyed, and because they love their son, they sent him to planet Earth in a spaceship to save his life. He was just an infant when they did this. He was found by the Kent family and raised as a normal human being. When Kea-El grew up and became a young man, he was increasingly aware of his unique strength.

He set off on a quest to discover who he really is. In his pursuit, he discovered a green piece of crystal in the ship that brought him to earth. Kea-El, now called Superman, was led by an internal voice to the North Pole where he simply threw the crystal and it opened a time portal. His father spoke to him from his past and told him everything he needed to know about who he is. Though his father was long since gone, he spoke life and purpose into his son. Superman wears a fitted outfit that has a large S on the chest of the outfit.

I always thought the "S" stood for Superman. When I watched the movie later, I learned the "S" stood for hope. Hope has always been, and will always be, what people need. When we lose hope, we lose the ability to thrive in life. Hope gives us the strength to endure and persevere. Hope is spiritual fuel to keep going. Hope, in as much as the presence of hope, is vital to help us press on; the absence of hope can be devastating, as the wisdom writer warned us: "Hope postponed grieves the heart; but when a dream comes true, life is full and sweet" (Proverbs 13:12 VOICE)

Humans are not time travelers, and Superman is not a real person. As it occurred in the movie, however, we too can speak into our descendants and tell them who they are and where they came from, all because God is guiding us, so we can love, encourage, affirm and guide them even from a distance.

In Genesis, we read where after Cain killed his brother Abel, the Lord comes and inquires of Cain concerning his actions.

> Then the LORD said to Cain, "Where is Abel your brother?" He said, "I do not know. Am I my brother's keeper?" And He said, "What have you done? The voice of your brother's blood cries out to Me from the ground (Genesis 4:9-10)

We learn that the life source of Abel, which was his blood, still spoke out even after he was dead. My desire is also to speak to my family, and to send love and life to them, even after I have transitioned. When we see the Bible as the eternal blueprint for life, then we believe that we also have the same God that the prophets of old had. Likewise, the same blessings given them are given to us. Our current technology has made this even more possible. In a hundred years there's no telling what the communication venues will be. There are many things we possess today they we saw as fiction in our past that has now become our reality. Dick Tracey was a cartoon character super spy who talked into his wristwatch walkie talkie, today we talk into Apple I-Watches.

It's an amazing thing to be able to communicate through time and space. In this current time, we have writings, videos, and audio recordings—all these and even more ways to still speak. We have access to great technology, and an amazing God!

You Are Extraordinary

ONE OF THE first things we learn about God from the Bible is that He is a creator. Almost the entire book of Genesis is about His creative nature. Everything in the entire known world on earth, beneath the earth, and above the earth was made by God. We need to understand His amazing creative powers so we can understand the things around us. It helps us understand that nothing gets past God. There is no hidden thing of which He is not aware. Likewise, there is nothing He doesn't know all about. He is God omniscient.

> Question: "What does it mean that God is omniscient?"
> Answer: (According to the website *Got Questions* (*www.gotquestions.org/God-omniscient.html*), it means possessed of universal or complete knowledge; the omniscient God.

I found this to be of great significance in my life. I needed to embrace that whatever was going on in my life, God knew all about it and He was still in control. This truth held true not only in obvious things, but also the not-so-obvious ones. I know there are others in this world who are much smarter, much prettier, and much more anointed than I. It's for all these reasons, I am humbled and honored that God has called me to prepare this legacy for you.

God knows that you will be extraordinary! He already knows everything there is to know about you. He has such great plans for you. He's commissioned me to leave this legacy for you so that you will know He has you on His mind before you were even born. Personally, I think that's super exciting. Even though this writing is coming through me, its actual author is God. He's the master builder and He's put some amazing gifts, talents, and anointing in you! He wants you to know that you are not common, average, or insignificant. You may sometimes feel strange like you don't fit in with the crowd, and that's good! Those are indications that you're becoming aware of your uniqueness. Remember, being extraordinary does not make you better than anyone else. On the contrary, it makes you a servant to all the others.

One of my favorite Scriptures was always Psalms 139 (we'll expound on this later), but it is such a clear indication that Gods has had you in His sight from time before your time. This intimate knowledge is not exclusively for you, but He has known every man. The prophet Jeremiah spoke to this intimate knowledge: "Then the word of the LORD came to me, saying: 'Before I formed you in the womb I knew you; before you were born I sanctified you; I ordained you a prophet to the nations'" (Jeremiah 1:4-5)

I'm also excited about this Scripture text because Jeremiah did not know or was not aware of the purpose for which God had created him. What's more, Jeremiah was a young man. This lets me know there's no age limit to this discovery of God's purpose.

What I also take away from this text is that our bodies were built to house our gifts. At times, people go on a quest looking outwardly for their purpose, which was in them all the while. This is what gives continuity to meditation as we learn to sit quietly before the Lord. When we get quiet, we can hear Him speak through the still small voice within us. A life of frustration and disappointment is a life where you never found out who you were created to be. On the other side of the coin, a life that finds purpose and lives it accordingly is a life rich with fulfillment and gratification.

I believe that *you* are extraordinary! In fact, I'm convinced of it! I also believe that's why God had me write you this legacy, so you would know it, too. I believe that you will discover your purpose and gifts. At the time I wrote this, many of you, my grandchildren, are infants and toddlers and, like Jeremiah, some have not even been conceived. I find it intriguing that I look at you now as babies, but I am also aware that there is so much more inside of you than I can imagine. I'm excited about the purpose and God's plan for you, and for your children! Extraordinary, you are!

God Knows You Inside Out

I'M CERTAIN ALL my family knows full well that I am called to be a preacher of the gospel, the good news. Over my lifetime, the Holy Spirit has given me thousands of sermons, and as much as I'd love to preach them all to you, I won't. I do, however, will share just a few messages later in this writing that I have preached that I feel speak to the core of who we are. Whether male or female, we know that God knows us explicitly, and He can speak to the person inside of us even when we aren't even aware of who that person is. This is Psalm 139 opening us up and talking to us personally. Inside every physical body lives a spiritual body. That's an amazing thing to know and even more amazing thing when you meet the spirit-being inside of you. We believe that this spirit-being existed long before the flesh-and-blood being did: "I knew you before you were formed within your mother's womb; before you were born I sanctified you and appointed you as my spokesman to the world" (Jeremiah 1:5 TLB)

There is a children's Disney movie that was even a written

book called *Inside Out* (https://movies.disney.com/inside-out). It's about a young girl who moved to a new city with her family, and the change prompted many challenges for her. Riley is uprooted from her Midwest life and moved to San Francisco, where her emotions—joy, fear, anger, disgust, and sadness—produce a conflict as to how best to navigate the new city. Even though Riley is a fictitious character, we also struggle with our emotions and other thoughts in our mind that are trying to lead and control our direction.

Certainly, our thoughts or emotions are not all bad, but they're not all good either. It's what we call a mixed bag. God gave us all our emotions and our brain, but sometimes our free will takes over and leads us in ways that are not God's will for us. The mind is often the place where the enemy directs his greatest attacks. The mind is the place where we rationalize our thoughts and cause or birth our actions. When we think we are wise in our own sight, we often fool only ourselves. Mental illness is real. It must also be dealt with to the same measure as any physical illness. To ignore mental illness is a grave mistake that you must not commit:

- If you live your life animated by the flesh—namely, your fallen, corrupt nature—then your mind is focused on the matters of the flesh. But if you live your life animated by the Spirit—namely, God's indwelling presence—then your focus is on the work of the Spirit. A mind focused on the flesh is doomed to death, but a mind focused on the Spirit will find full life and complete peace (Romans 8:5-6 Voice)

- Let us begin. The worship of the Eternal One, the one True God, is the first step toward knowledge. Fools, however, do not fear God and cannot stand wisdom or guidance (Proverbs 1:7 Voice)

- Those who love discipline love knowledge, but fools hate any kind of correction (Proverbs 12:1 VOICE)

The Word tells us we need to have the mind of Christ, so we can have the life He came to give us. There was a slogan often spoken in our era, "A mind is a terrible thing to waste." The purpose of this saying was:

The UNCF, also known as the United Negro College Fund was incorporated in 1944 by Frederick D. Patterson (then president of what is now Tuskegee University). It is an American philanthropic organization that funds scholarships for black students and general scholarship funds for 37 private historically black colleges and universities.

In 2005, UNCF supported approximately 65,000 students at over 900 colleges and universities with approximately $113 million in grants and scholarships. About 60% of these students were the first in their families to attend college, and 62% have annual family incomes of less than $25,000. UNCF also administers over 450 named scholarships. This has been the slogan of the United Negro College Fund since 1972. Education can still be the driving force to guide young and old alike, not to waste the gift called the mind. I know many of you will attend colleges. I also know some of you may not. Either way, always utilize your gifts and commit your mind to the will of God and the plan that He has for your life. There is a perfect plan for you, and you have everything you need to accomplish it. "A mind is a still a terrible thing to waste". Don't waste too much time and please, don't waste your brain power; your mind.

Psalm 139

O Lord, You have searched me and known me.
You know my sitting down and my rising up;
You understand my thought afar off.
You comprehend my path and my lying down,
And are acquainted with all my ways.
For there is not a word on my tongue,
But behold, O Lord, You know it altogether.
You have hedged me behind and before,
And laid Your hand upon me.
Such knowledge is too wonderful for me;
It is high, I cannot attain it.
Where can I go from Your Spirit?
Or where can I flee from Your presence?
If I ascend into heaven, You are there;
If I make my bed in hell, behold, You are there.
If I take the wings of the morning,
And dwell in the uttermost parts of the sea,
Even there Your hand shall lead me,
And Your right hand shall hold me
If I say, "Surely the darkness shall fall on me,"
Even the night shall be light about me;
Indeed, the darken shall not hide from You,
ut the night shines as the day;
The darkness and the light are both alike to You.
For You formed my inward parts;
You covered me in my mother's womb.
I will praise You, for I am fearfully and wonderfully made;
Marvelous are Your works,

And that my soul knows very well.
My frame was not hidden from You,
When I was made in secret,
And skillfully wrought in the lowest parts of the earth.
Your eyes saw my substance, being yet unformed.
And in Your book they all were written,
The days fashioned for me,
When as yet there were none of them.
How precious also are Your thoughts to me, O God!
How great is the sum of them!
If I should count them, they would be
more in number than the sand;
When I awake, I am still with You.
Oh, that You would slay the wicked, O God!
Depart from me, therefore, you blood thirsty men.
For they speak against You wickedly;
Your enemies take Your name in vain.
Do I not hate them, O LORD, who hate You?
And do I not loathe those who rise up against You?
I hate them with perfect hatred;
I count them my enemies.
Search me, O God, and know my heart;
Try me, and know my anxieties;
And see if there is any wicked way in me,
And lead me in the way everlasting.
Matthew Henry's Commentary Bible Gateway online
concerning this song of David says this;

Some of the Jewish doctors are of opinion that this is
the most excellent of all the psalms of David; and a

very pious devout meditation it is upon the doctrine of God's omniscience, which we should therefore have our hearts fixed upon and filled with in singing this psalm. This doctrine is here asserted, and fully laid down, (Ps. 139:1-6). It is confirmed by two arguments 1. God is everywhere present; therefore he knows all, (Ps. 139:7-12). 2. He made us, therefore he knows us, (Ps. 139:13-16). This great and self-evident truth, That God knows our hearts, and the hearts of all the children of men, if we did but mix faith with it and seriously consider it and apply it, would have a great influence upon our holiness and upon our comfort.

(Note: Scriptures in parenthesis are the commentary guide to where in the Scripture they are referring to.)

I concur with this commentary and its perception of David's song. The thread that ties this entire song together is that God is omniscient; He knows everything. It helps us to know this to be true about God's character for two reasons. One, we need to see His authority over us because He fully knows us inside and out, and second, we need to see also how He demonstrated His agape love towards us by still dying for us. I recall a greeting card that I received once that stated, "A good friend is someone who knows everything about you, and they still love you." God is the friend that sticks even closer to us then our brother.

Another God characteristic revealed in this song is God is omnipresent.

Definition of **OMNIPRESENT**: "present in all places at all times." (Merriam-Webster Dictionary).

David realizes that there is nowhere that he can go that God is not there. That's also a powerful truth we must embrace about God's nature, so we never feel like we are outside of His reach. Another God characteristic is that He is eternal—He is forever. We often say He's the Alpha and Omega. This is powerful for many reasons because He will never stop being God. He's inexhaustible. I am again grateful for this characteristic, because since this legacy will extend to a thousand generations, the Word will not have changed one bit. What that translates to is this: God's Word is God and neither He nor His word will ever change. There are a lot of things that will go out of style, but the holy Bible won't be one of them "For I am the LORD, I do not change; therefore you are not consumed, O sons of Jacob (Malachi 3:6) and "I am the Alpha and the Omega, the Beginning and the End," says the Lord, "who is and who was and who is to come, the Almighty" (Revelation 1:8)

David wrote this song to remind himself, as well as us, that the Sovereign God, the Creator of everything, the Ruler and Redeemer, knows all there is to know about us. He knows every word and every deed. His hand was the one that knit us into the womb of our mother. All that we know about ourselves, He knows more. There is never a time that we could keep a secret from God; He knows even our thoughts. He waits for us to come to Him, so He can reveal so many wonderful things to us—things that will sometimes blow our minds because we can't even imagine the things, He wants to tell us about us. Prayer is the way we talk to God, and fellowship in the Holy Spirit along with studying His Word are how He answers.

Yes, You Can Pray

WE HAVE TALKED many times already in this book about being led by God by having an intimate and personal relationship with Him. I must be clear that this does not just happen by a hocus-pocus magic trick or by attending church or singing in the choir. You can put lots of money in the offering, and be president of a ministry, but that won't do it either. These are all good things to do, but none of them are equal to a relationship with God. Those activities would be more valuable and spiritual if done *because* you have a relationship with Him, and prayer is critical to having a relationship with the Lord. A relationship with God without a prayer life is like the sun without the heat, or the oceans without water. I wrote a book on prayer and I'm going to share some of the thoughts and verses I used in that writing.

No prayer, no power. Little prayer, little power, Much prayer, much power. Prayer is one of the simple, yet mighty gifts and privileges we have been given, and we must use it if we want to have the abundant life that Jesus died to give us. The Bible is full of prayer, and we could spend a lot of time studying every prayer and what it yielded, so let's take a brief overview of the power, purpose, and necessity of prayer: "Then He spoke a parable to them, that men always ought to pray and not lose heart" (Luke 18:1)

Prayer is a privilege, not a prerogative. It is not to be taken lightly or without regarding that we even have the privilege to pray. Consider that prayer is an opportunity for sinful men and women to communicate with the holy God, he Creator of heaven and earth, the sovereign One, Elohim, Yahweh, Jehovah God, the eternal Spirit and El-Shaddai. God revealed Himself in the times past by the things that He would do, so the early people would call His name by His behaviors or His characteristics. We also call Him by His many names when we pray. He's Healer, Redeemer, Deliverer, My Shepperd, Living Water, Bread of Heaven…

Because of God's holiness, we would have never been able to speak with Him, but because He loves us so much, He provides a way and that way is a man and His name is Jesus. He gives us access to a righteous God when we come under His righteousness, for we are sinners, but He knew no sin. Jesus is now mediator between Holy God and sinful mankind and that is how we now have access granted instead of access denied.

Prayer is a dialogue, not a monologue. Because we now live under the dispensation of grace whereby, we have access to God, we can take this privilege for granted and lose sight of the holy God as we focus more on ourselves and what we need or want Him to do for us. It is common for prayer to start as we think of ourselves, but when we truly enter His presence in our prayer, we will feel a shift in our emphasis from us to Him. He is good, loving, patient, able, and faithful.

- And the LORD said to him: "I have heard your prayer and your supplication that you have made before Me; I have consecrated this house which you have built to put My name there forever, and My eyes and My heart will be there perpetually" (1 Kings 9:3)

- "Then the LORD appeared to Solomon by night, and said to him: "I have heard your prayer, and have chosen this place for Myself as a house of sacrifice. When I shut up heaven and there is no rain, or command the locusts to devour the land, or send pestilence among My people, if My people who are called by My name will humble themselves, and pray and seek My face, and turn from their wicked ways, then I will hear from heaven, and will forgive their sin and heal their land. Now My eyes will be open and My ears attentive to prayer *made* in this plac" (2 Chronicles 7:12-15)

- "But certainly God has heard *me*; He has attended to the voice of my prayer. Blessed *be* God, Who has not turned away my prayer, Nor His mercy from me!" (Psalm 66:19-20)

- "The LORD is far from the wicked, but He hears the prayer of the righteous (Proverbs 15:29)

- "For this child I prayed, and the LORD has granted me my petition which I asked of Him" (1 Samuel 1:27)

- "For I know the thoughts that I think toward you, says the LORD, thoughts of peace and not of evil, to give you a future and a hope.Then you will call upon Me and go and pray to Me, and I will listen to you" (Jeremiah 29:11-12)

- "When my soul fainted within me, I remembered the LORD; And my prayer went *up* to You, Into Your holy temple (Jonah 2:7)

- "For the eyes of the LORD are on the righteous, And His ears are open to their prayers; But the face of the LORD is against those who do evil" (1 Peter 3:12)

- "And when you pray, you shall not be like the hypocrites. For they love to pray standing in the synagogues and on the corners of the streets, that they may be seen by men. Assuredly, I say to you, they have their reward. But you, when you pray, go into your room, and when you have shut your door, pray to your Father who *is* in the secret *place*; and your Father who sees in secret will reward you openly. And when you pray, do not use vain repetitions as the heathen *do*. For they think that they will be heard for their many words. Therefore do not be like them. For your Father knows the things you have need of before you ask Him. In this manner, therefore, pray: Our Father in heaven, Hallowed be Your name" (Matthew 6:5-9)

- "Watch and pray, lest you enter into temptation. The spirit indeed *is* willing, but the flesh *is* weak." Again, a second time, He went away and prayed, saying, "O My Father, if this cup cannot pass away from Me unless I drink it, Your will be done." And He came and found them asleep again, for their eyes were heavy. So He left them, went away again, and prayed the third time, saying the same words (Matthew 26:41-44)

- "Husbands, likewise, dwell with them with understanding, giving honor to the wife, as to the weaker vessel, and as being heirs together of the grace of life, that your prayers may not be hindered" (1 Peter 3:7)

As I stated earlier, the Bible is filled with prayers—some long and some short but all are prayers. The merit of the prayer is measured by the content of the heart, so as you read through these different prayers, remember they were from all kinds of people in all kinds of different situations, but your prayer is your prayer. We can glean from others' prayer or even use their model prayer as a guide, but you have your own prayer to pray. Many of us have brought Hallmark greeting cards to express our feelings of love, gratitude, or even sympathy.

Hallmark has a wonderful way of expressing our feelings, but at some point in time, you must speak for yourself. Prayer is the same way. Many other prayers may sound good to our ear, and say the things we also feel, but at some point in time, you must talk to God for yourself. He's waiting to hear from you, not just about you. Yes, you can pray, and you will pray. Pray this prayer now

> *Dear Lord, please teach me how to pray. Teach me, Lord, how to hear Your desires for me and how to posture my prayer in agreement with Your will. Lord, lead me by Your Spirit s I may move by Your guidance into my place with You. I love you, Lord, and my heart's desire is to live my life pleasing to You. Teach me, Oh Lord, Your ways and I will follow. I need you every step of the way, lead me and guide me my God, my Strength, and my Redeemer. Hallelujah to Your name.*

"We must remember the goal of prayer is the ear of God. Unless that is gained, the prayer has utterly failed. The uttering of it may have kindled devotional feeling in our minds, the hearing of it may have comforted and strengthened the hearts of those with whom we have prayed, but if the prayer has not gained the heart of God, it has failed in its essential purpose." – Charles Spurgeon

I want to take the term *prayer* and exchange it for the word, *communicate*. I want this not to be a religious approach but more of a universal way that people exchange information and ideals. As human beings, we will always need to communicate with one another. Even the cries of an infant are a communication that the child has needs to be met. In every relationship you are involved in, you will need to communicate. We must also understand effective communication is comprised of both speaking and listening. When both or all parties speak and listen, it is a dialogue. It is very important to learn to listen. This is true whether with your spouse, your child, your boss, or the divine God. The saying is that we have one mouth and two ears, we should do twice as much listening as we do talking.

When we communicate with God, it's called prayer. There are some specific things about prayer that differ from communication with another person. First and foremost, God is not a man. He's the eternal Creator of all heaven, earth, and beneath the earth. Everything and everyone that exists, He made them.

When we pray to Him, we respect Him as a holy God. I remember hearing older folks saying when I was a young person, "You don't question God." As I grew older, however, I had a lot of questions for God, so I asked Him. Since God knows everything, and He sees my thoughts, He knew I had questions. The growth came for me when I learned to listen to Him as He answered my questions. That's prayer.

We don't need to imitate anyone else's prayer style or language. Each one of us can pray and communicate with God in our own unique way. He made us all different, so He'll be able to handle it.

Make prayer a regular part of your daily lifestyle. I promise this will help you in every aspect of your life. No prayer, no power. I believe little prayer, little power; much prayer; much power. There's an old song and the lyrics are, "Somebody prayed for me, had me on their mind. Took a little time and prayed for me. I'm so glad they prayed. I'm so glad they prayed, I'm so glad they prayed for me." Well, I want you to know that I prayed for you and I had you on my mind.

Heavenly Father,

I thank You so very much for the person who right now is reading this prayer; I thank You, Lord, that You laid the desire upon my heart to consider my future generations and to speak to them. I thank You, Lord, that You knew them before they were even born, and You love them. I pray they will learn to both talk and listen to You. I know You have a plan and a purpose for their lives that they may not yet know. I pray for their hearts to be kind and open. I pray that their minds will be covered by Your hand. I pray that they know what it is to experience love. I pray they will understand that their gifts and talents were given to them to serve others and not themselves exclusively. I pray they learn true worship. I'm certain some of them You will call into ministry. Thank you, Lord. I pray, Lord, that they live with integrity and morals, and that they respect all people. I pray they learn to disagree, agreeably. My heart's prayer is they will someday be called men and women of God. Thank You, Lord.

Your Key

[19] *"And that's not all. You will have complete and free access to God's kingdom, keys to open any and every door: no more barriers between heaven and earth, earth and heaven. A yes on earth is yes in heaven. A no on earth is no in heaven." Matthew 16:19 The Message (MSG)*

IN 2017 GOD gave me a profound revelation about this scripture. When I think of a key I think of an instrument to gain access. A key is a tangible object, most time held in our hand and inserted into a lock of some kind. As we know there are numerous styles and shapes of keys as there are various locks. We also know every key won't open every lock. Keys are designed specifically to open a specific lock. So just having a key is not the guarantee to gain access if it's not for the certain lock.

In time the keys have progressed from being just a metal object to being a series of numbers and alpha characters; to even the pupils

of your eyes. The key has evolved to become more and more intricate
and complex.

> And I will give you the keys of the kingdom of heaven,
> and whatever you bind on earth will be bound in
> heaven, and whatever you loose on earth will be loosed
> in heaven." Matthew 16:19 (NKJV)

The text speaks that Jesus will give us the keys to unlock the
things of heaven. What would the things in heaven be? Perhaps
they would be the gifts and fruits of the Holy Spirit; Joy, love, peace,
patience, hope, comfort, perseverance, temperance, power, authority,
divine purpose, discernment, healing, power over demons, wisdom,
knowledge, faith, prophesy, miracles, speaking in diverse tongues and
the interpretation of tongues.

When God gave me a revelation on this scripture, He told me
that we don't have to obtain the key, that we in fact *are* the key. Each
one of us is uniquely designed and created by God with specific
intricate detail in us. Everything about us is a custom design, no two
designs are alike, not even twins.

God knows every minute derail about us (Psalms 139). He knows
because He gave them to us. They extend from the nature of our
gender to the number of hairs upon our head.

This revelation of the access to heaven and the authority on earth
came after Peter had declared that by God's Spirit, He knew who the
Christ was.

*Simon Peter answered and said, "You are the Christ, the Son of
the living God."*

> [17] *Jesus answered and said to him, "Blessed are you,
> Simon Bar-Jonah, for flesh and blood has not revealed*

this to you, but My Father who is in heaven. Matthew 16:16-17

It is upon the knowing of who God is, that our keys become cut and shaped and re-designed to open the windows of heaven. That's what Jesus is telling Simon and telling us. We are born as a key, but a key that needed cut to fit the entry parts of heaven. The combination of the Father, the Son (Word) and the Spirit we are shaped and re-born and obtain authority in heaven and upon the earth. The key was always with us because the key is us.

We must willingly give ourselves back to the master locksmith and He will give us back access.

> *I beseech you therefore, brethren, by the mercies of God, that you present your bodies a living sacrifice, holy, acceptable to God, which is your reasonable service. ² And do not be conformed to this world, but be transformed by the renewing of your mind, that you may prove what is that good and acceptable and perfect will of God. Romans 12:1-2*

This year (2017) I met with each of my children and their spouse and I spoke life and affirmation into each of them as being different but valuable. I apologized for mistakes I made as their mother and I asked them not to make the same mistakes with their children. I gave each family a bottle of anointing oil to pray over their families and each person a unique key with a tag of this scripture written upon it. The key was something relevant to the person who received it. I also gave them a large Family picture frame with the *Family is the key* engraved upon it. I asked my children to promise me that they would speak affirmation of life into their children. I charged them to pass this key ministry down to their children as a legacy act of affirmation. Later, I made key charm bracelets for all the girls.

I pray that my children remember their promise and continue this legacy of life from generation to generation, and forever more.

The Value of Integrity

He who walks with integrity walks securely,
But he who perverts his ways will become known (Proverbs 10:9)

I WANT TO talk to you about a human characteristic that is critical to a quality life lived with morals and decency. In my lifetime, I have known many people, some personally, and some not, who had talents, or gifts, or wealth, but lacked integrity, and it was to their demise. You may very well be born with an amazing singing voice, or great athletic ability, but if you have no integrity, you have nothing. It won't be by the measure of your wealth, or the material possessions you obtain, or even by the seat of power you occupy, as to how men will perceive you or how God will judge you.

> Definition of **INTEGRITY:** Firm adherence to a code of especially moral or artistic values: INCORRUPTIBILITY (MERRIAM-WEBSTER DICTIONARY)

You can be a teacher, preacher, doctor, lawyer, garbage man, or bus driver, it matters not what you do, but rather how you do it. I have seen wealthy people commit unthinkable crimes. I've known of people who have had powerful positions, who could not remain faithful to their spouses. Many extremely successful people have ended up losing everything they had gained, and even more, because they operated under a mindset of entitlement and superiority, and the house of cards did eventually come tumbling down.

The Bible has much to say about mankind living and walking in Integrity. Here are a few of the scriptures that speak to this.

- "Now if you walk before Me as your father David walked, in *integrity* of heart and in uprightness, to do according to all that I have commanded you, and if you keep My statutes and My judgments, then I will establish the throne of your kingdom over Israel forever, as I promised David your father, saying, 'You shall not fail to have a man on the throne of Israel'" (1 Kings 9:4-5, emphasis added)
- Then the LORD said to Satan, "Have you considered My servant Job, that there is none like him on the earth, a blameless and upright man, one who fears God and shuns evil? And still he holds fast to his *integrity*, although you incited Me against him, to-destroy him without cause" (Job 2:3)
- Far be it from me That I should say you are right; Till I die I will not put away my *integrity* from me (Job 27:5)
- Let me be weighed on honest scales, That God may know my *integrity* (Job 31:6)

o The Lord shall judge the peoples; Judge me, O Lord, according to my righteousness, And according to my *integrity* within me (Psalm 7:8)

o [The Fear of the Lord Leads to Life] Better is the poor who walks in his *integrity* Than one who is perverse in his lips, and is a fool (Proverbs 19:1)

o The righteous man walks in his *integrity*; His children are blessed after him (Proverbs 20:7)

o Better is the poor who walks in his *integrity* Than one perverse in his ways, though he be rich (Proverbs 28:6)

o Likewise, exhort the young men to be sober-minded, in all things showing yourself to be a pattern of good works; in doctrine showing *integrity*, reverence, incorruptibility sound speech that cannot be condemned, that one who is an opponent may be ashamed, having nothing evil to say of you (Titus 2:6-8)

It has been said that integrity is not how you behave when people are watching you, but rather how you behave when no one is watching you. Like most characteristics, living a life of integrity is a choice. Many times, people have done things that were not good, and since no one saw them, they felt like they had gotten away with them. When you are a man or woman of integrity, you always consider that God sees everything, and there really is no getting away with it—whatever it is. When you live without integrity, you live without peace. When you have no peace, hope is also far from you. When hope is far from you, then the power to believe is diminished. If morals were a thermometer, then integrity would be the highest achievable measure on it. When you choose to have integrity, this doesn't mean you'll be perfect. Quite the contrary, it means you work hard to improve your imperfections.

I watched a TV talk show one morning, *CBS News* (September 3, 2018), and the guest was Yuval Noah Harari, an Israeli historian and author of *Sapiens* and *Homo Deus*. He spoke about what the future will look like in approximately fifty years. He stated that with the continual progression of AI (artificial intelligence), there is going to be many immeasurable changes and shifts in the economy, job market, government, and power systems. In his current book, *21 Lessons for the 21st Century*, he presents the fact that people are going to need to be agile and flexible enough to recreate themselves multiple times within their lifetime. Harari, along with other experts in his field, indicate that currently the educational systems are not teaching future generations how to prepare for this. They will need to know how to manage their emotional intelligence, so they are flexible to all the changes they will have to endure. We are witnessing even now what the technological enhancements have contributed to our culture. They are neither good nor bad, but what will make them either is the hand that guide them. He used the example that AI and biotechnology, which can be used to create a paradise or a hell—it's up to us.

The reason I'm bringing this up is I am giving you a heads up. You will no doubt be living in a reality that when I wrote this legacy, those things we only imagined, now will exist in your lifetime. These are very credible people who see the storm coming. I want to speak to you to be prepared. Don't get in your own way. Do all that you can to keep your mind sound! This is one of the reasons you want to have an intimate relationship with God. He promises to keep your mind in the place of peace when you are in relationship with Him.

> Be anxious for nothing, but in everything by prayer and supplication, with thanksgiving, let your requests be made known to God; and the peace of God, which surpasses all understanding, will guard your hearts and minds through Christ Jesus (Philippians 4:6-7)

The mind of the man is likened to the steering wheel in a car. It is the controlling force for direction. I used to say that if a man thinks himself to be a monkey; he will spend all his time looking for bananas and trees. This is why the enemy often attacks your mind. He knows that if he can control your mind, he controls you. I don't think for one moment that people with mental illness wanted to be ill any more than a person with cancer would want to have cancer. I do, however, think we must take responsibility for the things we can, and then do all we can to protect and defend them. God gave us a body, a heart, and a mind so He could dwell in them. It sometimes takes us a long time, even a lifetime, to figure out what that really means.

You can be healthy, wealthy, and strong, but if you lose your mind, it's all for naught. So, we must guard our mind with God's Word. I have a pastor friend whose son went off to college, and at a party someone put a drug in his drink that attacked his mind. This young man's life has been forever changed because of one drink. He didn't see this attack coming but God sees everything, and by His Holy Spirit He will lead and guide and protect us. In 2018, this young man died. Before that, his life had become a series of mental and emotional challenges that he could not overcome.

Biography

I WANT YOU to know who I am. It may or may not help you to understand who you are, for that's yet to be decided. I was the fifth child born to Helen (West) Dennis and Raymond Dennis on June 3, 1959 at Pittsburgh Hospital. My siblings are Raymond Dennis Jr., Andrea (Coleman – Betts) Dennis, Marilyn (Jones-Taliaferro) Dennis, and Stephen Dennis. I had a good childhood and my mother was a great mother. After she divorced my father, she raised her five children as a single mother and did a great job. We always celebrated holidays, went on vacations, and had birthday parties.

We all attended the local school, Burgwin Elementary, which all my children also attended when they were growing up; then Justin, returned to as a faculty member. My education was Burgwin, Mifflin Middle School, Taylor Allderdice High School, and I graduated from Schenley High School in 1977. I later went to several colleges, Carlow College and Allegheny Community College. Once I was called into ministry, I attended and finished American Baptist Theological

Seminary, and later took several classes at Geneva College (Center for Urban Biblical Ministries).

On May 23, 1981, I married Brian Ericson Peeks, who was one of my high school sweethearts. We had three children, Delvin Ericson Peeks (12.22.1978), Justin Lee Peeks (5.24.1984), and Jasmin Rae Peeks (3.6.1988). Brian was a great father to his children, whom he loved immensely, but he had other problems that eventually led to our divorce on November 12, 1993. Even though we divorced, Brian remained a significant part of his children's lives until his accidental death (10.3.2000). I had a unique life, since I later married my other high school sweetheart.

On September 30, 2000, I was united in holy matrimony to David Kevin Jeffries. Uniquely, Brian, David, and I all attended Taylor Allderdice High School, and we were all friends one with another. There was a New Year's Day I will never forget. I still lived at home and both Brian and David decided to drop in to see me, although neither had been invited. Of course, it became awkward and David left, and then Brian left, but then Brian came back. Well, the rest was history.

I remain married to David, who is now Deacon David Jeffries, and the chairman of our deacon board. He has two children of his own, David Kevin Jeffries Jr (DJ) and Toy Williams. We never had any children together, but he has been a good stepfather to our children and has contributed to them being the adults they have become. He has loved them and our grandchildren just like they were his own birth children. Thank You, Lord.

I worked several jobs up until I was hired by Highmark Blue Cross in March of 1978. I remained at Highmark until I was offered to participate in a voluntary termination program, which the company had never offered in the history of the organization, it was divine favor for me, in February 2009. I left that employment in April of the same year with thirty-two years of service. This job separation was an act of God, for I was only fifty years young. The Lord brought me out with His strong arm, hallelujah!

In January of 1999, the Lord called me into ministry. He called me by His word found in Ephesians:

> (Now this, "He ascended"—what does it mean but that He also first descended into the lower parts of the earth? He who descended is also the One who ascended far above all the heavens, that He might fill all things.) And He Himself gave some to be apostles, some prophets, some evangelists, and some pastors and teachers, for the equipping of the saints for the work of ministry, for the edifying of the body of Christ, till we all come to the unity of the faith and of the knowledge of the Son of God, to a perfect man, to the measure of the stature of the fullness of Christ (Ephesians 4:9-13)

I was licensed in the gospel ministry (this is being sanctioned by your church pastor to preach and teach the Bible under his or her instruction) in June 1999 at Morning Star Baptist Church at 5524 Second Avenue in Pittsburgh under my pastor and father in ministry; Reverend Malachi Smith. I was ordained in November of the same year at the same location. The ordination process is a much more intense procedure during which the candidate goes before a counsel of already ordained preachers who ask a number of questions. After the intense questioning to verify a working knowledge of the Bible and the foundational truths of the faith, then there is a full service of ordination or validation and acceptance of the candidate. This credentialing gives power to the preacher to perform marriages and committals of deceased persons. The candidate is then also permitted to serve the communion of the Lord's Supper.

While I was at Morning Star, I began several ministries of my own. I founded a ministry called Sister/Sista. This was a ministry for women preachers from all churches for teaching in the Word, female etiquette, and fellowship amongst sisters. This ministry lasted more than fifteen years, and in 2017, we rebranded and reinvented, and are now named Na' Omi, Inc. We are a ministry where wisdom and maturity lead and guide youth and energy, until both are positioned into purpose. This ministry is still in existence and we have partnered with local outreach programs to serve and support their outreaches. While at Morning Star, I also partnered with a local preacher, Reverend Cora Suiter, to embark on a radio ministry. I began a radio ministry "All About the Kingdom," and soon after, I started a television ministry "He that Hath an Ear," at PCTV-21. At the time of this writing, I still maintain my television show and have since 2008.

I love to do things with my hands, and so another ministry I enjoy is "In His Presence." I learned how to make candles, because I personally love them, but my signature with my candles and I anoint every jar with anointing oil and then I pray over every candle before I pour the wax. I also created several additional items (30-day devotionals, journals, mugs, pens, and prayer shawls from Israel), all to contribute to the heart that desires to be In His presence. I've also learned to make beaded jewelry, and these hobbies would often help me to calm myself down and relax. I have done some writing, 30 Day Devotionals, *Leading a Child to Christ* and *The Tree of Life*, but this will be my first published piece of literature. I have another ministry the Lord gave me with a key. I really love this ministry too, and I hope that you may already know about the key, because my desire was that it would be a part of your legacy handed down from your parents as I made them promise they would do. I'll talk more about the key later.

In the summer of 2005, I was called to pastor the First Baptist Church of North Vandergrift. In November of the same year, I was installed. This process is done by the church membership holding meetings and establishing a pulpit committee when there is no longer a pastor over the church. After having numerous visiting preachers come to preach and teach, they narrow the candidates down to a select few. In my case, I was the sole candidate who the committee chose to consider as the pastor of the church. This was not a status quo scenario, because women were still not readily received into ministry and certainly not to the office of pastor.

I was officially installed into the office of pastor on Sunday, November 6, 2005. My mother in ministry, Reverend Earlene Coleman, pastor of Bethlehem Baptist Church in McKeesport, PA, preached the morning service and my father in ministry, Reverend Malachi Smith, Morning Star Baptist Church, preached the afternoon service. The number of people who came to that installation was unbelievable. There were at least three hundred supporters, family, and friends who came out.

I cried the entire day. In fact, I cried for years every year on the anniversary of my installation. It is so humbling to think that God calls us to do this life-changing ministry of preaching the gospel message, I never saw this call to preach and pastor coming. My life, as I knew it, would never be the same. The church was a quaint, small, traditional, family-run church. Well, it didn't stay that way after God sent me there. I promise you it was God who sent me, because looking to be a pastor was the farthest thing from my mind. I quickly learned that God's mind is high above our minds.

I had been the pastor of First Baptist Church for five years, which then relocated and was renamed to New Life Baptist Church in Apollo, PA, and I remain the pastor today (June 2019). We have encountered numerous changes and a lot of growth in our church, and the Lord has remained faithful to us. I will share a few of my sermons (see the sermon Expressions) I have been blessed to preach/teach while I've been a preacher. Again, I say, thank You, Lord. God has been amazingly faithful to me and our family over these years. I'm certain you will know that for yourself in time.

Last, but not least, my favorite color is orange. I have a strong personality. I'm very intentional and deliberate. I'm jovial and I love traveling. I'm anointed, gifted and chosen. I love, love, love my family! I am daughter, sister, wife, mother, cousin, auntie, Nana, and pastor. I love who I am!

Charles- Ida Davis   Braxton – Nannie West

William – Isabella Peeks   Joseph Clyde --   Frank—Rebecca   John – Palma West
                            Lolene Woodson   Dennis

      Charles   ------- S. Yvonne Peeks   Raymond   ------- Helen Dennis

         Brian Peeks   ---------------------------- June Dennis

Delvin & Brandi Peeks   *Justin & Alexandria Peeks*   *Terence & Jasmin Harvey*

    Dalen Ericson   Marquis Nimar   Royal Rae
    Leah Michelle   Austin Franklin   Harmony Rain
                                 Liam Alexander   King Jaron
                                 Graysen Leigh

Facts

I want to give you some of the facts concerning your family. This is not in any way a full family legacy search but it's just the dates and names of some of the people who you are descendant of. Many of your grands and great- grand's marriages have several children to their unions but I will only give you the name of your direct lineage. Feel free to dig further into your heritage if you feel so inclined. I will indicate wedding dates, birthdate dates, and date of death where and if I have the info.

Brian Peeks and June Dennis married 5-23-1981. To that union were born, Delvin Ericson 12-22-1978, Justin Lee 5-24-1984 and Jasmin Rae 3-6-1988. Brian passed to an accidental death 10-3-2000. June remarried to David Jeffries 9-30-2000.

Delvin had a son, Dalen Ericson Peeks (Janelle Ross) born 1-2-2001. Delvin married Brandi Jones 10-3-2010 and that union was born Leah Michelle 3-22-2014.

Justin married Alexandria Fields 11-15-2008 who already had a son, Marquis Nimar born 10-30-2003, and to that union were born Austin Franklin 10-3-2010, Liam Alexander 7-10-2014 and Graysen Leigh 11-2-2017.

Jasmin was married to Terence Harvey 11-14-2015 and to that union were born, Royal Rae 9-7-2016, Harmony Rain 3-13-2018 and King Jaron 6-11-2019.

Brian was the middle child of five children of Charles and Yvonne Peeks; Darwin, Gary, Charvon and Breschell. June was the youngest of five children to Raymond and Helen Dennis; Raymond, Andrea, Marilyn and Stephen. Brian and June were divorced 11-12-1993.

Charles & Ida Davis

John R. West

Palma Carpenter West

Clyde & Lolene Woodson

Charles & Yvonne Peeks Wedding Day

Charles & Yvonne and children

Raymond & Helen Dennis Wedding Day

Helen Dennis with Raymond, Andrea, Marilyn, Stephen and June

Brian & June Peeks Wedding Day with Delvin

David & June Jeffries Wedding Day

Delvin & Brandi's Wedding Day

Justin & Alex's Wedding Day

Terence and Jasmin Harvey's Wedding Day

Delvin, Justin and Jasmin

Nana & crew Family Reunion

Delvin, Justin, Jasmin and Nana (Birthday 6.2018)

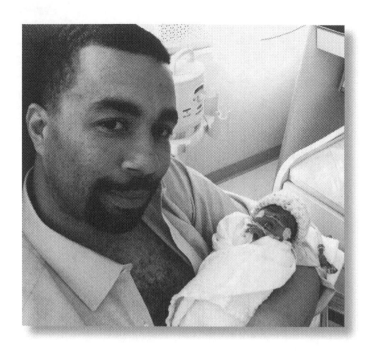

Our Miracle Leah & Daddy

Leah's coming home

Leah & Daddy

Austin & Daddy

Royal & Mommy

Nana & Jasmin at 50th birthday party

Justin, Jasmin, Delvin, Nana and Grandma

Royal & King

Jasmin, Alex and Brandi

Grandma Dennis, Nana, Jasmin Royal & Harmony (5.2018)

Delvin & Justin (5.2019)

Terence & Jasmin Harvey's Family

Terence & Jasmin and the girls

Harvey Family with King (6.2019)

Liam & Royal

Dalen, Grandma & Leah

Justin, Alex and family (12.2018)

Pappy & Nana Deer (12.2018)

Delvin, Brandi and family (12.2018)

Justin, Alex, Nana and family (Easter 2017)

Royal & Harmony Harvey

Nana & Pappy *Looking Good* (6.2018)

Grandma Peeks & Grandma Dennis

Grands on Nana's steps (12.2018)

Austin & King (7.2019)

Delvin & family Easter 2019

Justin & Alex Peeks

Grandma Peeks and family

Nana Wit

THERE'S AN OLD saying that we have referred to as Nana Wit. Nana Wit is expressions of wisdom, knowledge, or encouragement that people who have lived long enough to know something, speak to younger, less-experienced people. At this point in time (2019), you still have two living great grandmothers; Yvonne Peeks (85) and Helen Dennis (86) and also Pappy Jeffries (64) years young. I was so excited about sharing this legacy with them and asking them to share their wit with you.

> To grandchildren, great-grandchildren, and great-great-grandchildren, and on and on;
>
> What is it with the children today? You give them advice and they don't take it. We give them rules and they want to break them, but when it's all said and done, I love them dearly.

As you grow and mature and set your goals in life, remember always;

1. *Put God first*
2. *Pray daily*
3. *Read your Bible*

Whatever your concerns and problems are, stop worrying! Get out of the way. Let go and let God work on things.

The glory is not in never failing, but in rising every time you fall. If God had a wallet, your picture would be in it.

Whenever I count my blessings, there you are.

Keep smiling; it makes people wonder what you have been up to.

Clutter is found in so many shapes and sizes. We can find it on our kitchen table, under our beds, in our cars, and in our "heads". Keep your mind on your goals. Keep clutter out of your heads (8/16/2018).

My children, remember your roots. Your forefathers fought long and hard to gain little. Respect where you are today. Value their pain and suffering. Racism will be around for a long time.

Hold your head high and do your best in everything that you do. Put your trust in God. Listen to your elders. They have been around the jar and have seen the handle (8/30/2018).

Before you speak, ask yourself if what you are going to say is true, is kind, is necessary, and is helpful. If the answer is no, maybe what you are about to say should be left unsaid (9/21/2018).

Great Grandma Yvonne Peeks

Your Nana, June Jeffries, would have wanted for you to be happy and successful in all you do. Believe in God and believe in yourself. The Lord blessed your Nana in so many ways. You have also been blessed by the Lord. It will be good for you to bless forward to others. This is how you want to be known as a kind and giving person.

Great Grandma Helen Dennis

Have you ever gone on a road trip that seemed like it was going to be a long ride, and on the way, you fell asleep? When you awoke, you find out that a five-hour trip now has only an hour and a half left to go. This is pretty much like the road of life.

We can spend a lot of time just being nonproductive, which is just like being asleep. Don't let this happen to you. As a young person study hard, get a god education, and never think you're too old to learn more. Get a job you can enjoy and work hard for your money, but also be smart enough through savings and investing to let your money work just as hard for you.

We say that it takes a village to raise a child, but as the child gets older, they can forget some of the people in the village. A strong family can become an immoveable force in your life. A strong, godly family is a beacon that no matter where you are in your life, you can see and feel its presence.

Always remember nothing comes to a sleeper but a dream. Work to make your dreams a reality. With much love and prayer,

Pappy

Wise Words

- God given influence, is more the man-made affluence
- God created our body to house the anointing inside of us
- God can not lie , neither can He fail
- The road of life is liken to driving in a car. Utilize your windshield and pay attention to the side view mirrors and back window
- Your experience is always more than someone else's opinion
- Never be too pressed to say I love you and I'm sorry
- When you know more, you should do more; when you know better, you should do better
- Bloom where you're planted
- If you continue to try and eat soup with a fork, you'll remain frustrated and hungry.
- If you only do that which you can do , then you will never be more then you are
- They must kill your name before they kill you

- When you are young, you are a car with a full tank of gas but having no steering wheel. When maturity comes you have found your steering wheel however now your gas tank is half empty.
- The power of life and death is in your mouth. Speak Life.
- The bible is not a buffet table where you pick and choose to your liking
- Don't make permanent decisions under temporary circumstances
- You can soar in a flock, but you will fall alone
- Adhere is much more then to just hear
- Its time to get off the shoulders of your ancestors and stand on your own two feet

Psalm 78:1-8 (TLB)

O my people, listen to my teaching. Open your ears to what I am saying. For I will show you lessons from our history, stories handed down to us from former generations. I will reveal these truths to you so that you can describe these glorious deeds of Jehovah to your children and tell them about the mighty miracles he did. For he gave his laws to Israel and commanded our fathers to teach them to their children, so that they in turn could teach their children too. Thus his laws pass down from generation to generation. In this way each generation has been able to obey his laws and to set its hope anew on God and not forget his glorious miracles. Thus they did not need to be as their fathers were—stubborn, rebellious, unfaithful, refusing to give their hearts to God.

ONE TIME, I was on a spiritual contemplative retreat for females in ministry. This was a annual retreat event and I was always so very blessed in these times to just get quiet and hear from God. My dear friend, Reverend Dr. Joan Prentice (founder and pastor of Ephesus Project Ministry), who heads these retreats annually, was at this retreat, not as the lead, but more as a consultant. Pastor Joan has been a dear friend and co-laborer for years. The directive of this retreat was Gestalt Therapy. Gestalt therapy is a client-centered approach to <u>psychotherapy</u> that helps clients focus on the present and understand what is really happening in their lives right now, rather than what they may perceive to be happening based on past experience. Instead of simply talking about past situations, clients are encouraged to experience them, perhaps through re-enactment. Through the gestalt process, clients learn to become more aware of how their own negative thought patterns and behaviors are blocking true self-awareness and making them unhappy (Psychology Today). As we went through the exercises throughout the days, I began to feel like I didn't really have a deep hurt from which I needed healing. God does have a sense of humor, but He also has a plan and a purpose. Just before the time came for me to be ministered to, I really sought the Lord as to what did He wanted to address in me.

To my surprise, I simply took my journal and penned the word, *death*. I became transparent in my session and revealed that God had been pressing upon me to prepare for death. Not in a "get your house in order" kind of a way, but in a gentle and intentional way.

I wept because I felt so vulnerable, yet I knew what God was saying. Later that weekend, my dear friend gave me Psalm 78 to read. That was it! I have felt a push since then to set my legacy in order. When I read these words spoken by David, it was like he was talking straight to me. Now, I wept again, but this time with tears of gratitude and appreciation. This psalm was my instruction on what I was to do. I felt the sense of direction because I knew what He wanted. We say, "When you don't know where you're going, any road will get you there." Well, now I know where I'm going.

God has promised to lead and guide us by His Holy Spirit. We say that all the time, and we believe it, but when we see it played out, it is amazing. I feel like I was led to attend this retreat for the sole purpose of getting this psalm. When I think of all the ways the Lord has led me concerning this legacy journey, I know for certain I'm purposed to do this.

The Bible has numerous passages that instruct God's people to tell their children about the many wonderful things the Lord has done. There was always a great responsibility to hand down from one generation to the next and to the one after that about who God is: "Only take heed to yourself, and diligently keep yourself, lest you forget the things your eyes have seen, and lest they depart from your heart all the days of your life. And teach them to your children and your grandchildren" (Deuteronomy 4:9).

The Lord knew that when we stop telling our children about God, they would fall off from Him, and they have. The first classroom for our children is the home. It's in the home where they need to learn to pray and to read the Bible. They need to learn the children's Bible songs like *Yes, Jesus Loves Me*. Today, too many of our homes have put down the Bible and picked up a remote control or a game system control. Today, our children are not being brought to the church like in days of old. Today, so many parents ask the children what they want to do, as opposed to telling the children what they must do. The family is the first church. We used to say grace together around the dinner table and say prayers at bedtime before tucking the children into bed, but all these things are gone. When we deny our children the knowledge of God and His word, we handicap them in their living. There is no age too young to begin this exposure.

Much of what our young people are struggling with now are problems rooted in not having self-worth or self-esteem. These necessary characteristics come from knowing who they are in God. Additionally, having self-respect, obedience, temperance, honesty, and being moral also come from God. I have a real burden for young people. I love all the babies, and it really hurts my heart when people abuse or take advantage of them. The innocence of a child is precious in God's sight. When we are blessed to have children, the expectation is that we would love, protect, and provide for them. The sin that's running in this world has caused even parents to abuse their child, which is unthinkable, yet it happens all the time.

To My Dear Children

Dear Delvin,

MY FIRSTBORN CHILD. What can I say that you don't already know? I am as proud as any mother could be of you. I admit having the first child is where you have to learn what parenting really is. I won't use the word, experiment, but I'll say more trial and error (smiling and laughing). I never dropped you on your head, but I might have fallen down the steps trying to carry you and a load of laundry.

I still remember the day I took the pregnancy test. Back then, you had to go to a doctor's office. Miss Maria went with me and there it was, positive. *Here comes a baby.* I was elated. Though I don't condone pregnancy outside of marriage, I confess I do understand it. There is a time when a young woman just wants somebody to love on, and to have that same somebody love you back. I think that was where I was in my life. I remember your first kick, too. Aunt Lynn and I went to see the movie, *Grease*, at the Warner theatre on Fifth Ave, and when I was dancing with Olivia

Newton John in the movie finale, you started kicking. One might say, and you've been kicking ever since.

You were always smart and well-disciplined, too. I admit that I thought you were above average in your intelligence until I took you to the kindergarten assessment testing, and I quickly found out, all kids were smart. You were a great big brother and you even took on a paternal role very early. You were always telling Justin and Jasmin what to do and you did it from a position of authority, which you really didn't need to. I'm sure you're shocked to learn this.

I remember when you were in college, and I was a single mom at the time. You were on a scholarship and you may have done a work study job as well, but it occurred to me one day, you never called and asked me for anything. Now mind you, we didn't have much, but you never asked for any clothes, or care packages, or money.

I called and asked you; "Don't you ever need anything, Delvin?" You answered, "I'm okay, Mom. I'm fine". All these years later and I still feel like I'm about to cry just thinking about it. You didn't want to take anything off the table because you assessed that I was a single mother holding it all down by myself. I sent a box with things I figured you needed anyway, but it was your way to always want to be an asset and not a burden.

You are a good husband, father, brother and son, but your greatest asset is your strong faith in God. You still say "Yes, Mama" and you only want the best for all those you know. You have always made my proud to be your mother!

Love always,
Mommy

＊＊＊＊＊

-*HAPPY BIRTHDAY*-

Pass the light blue sky,
Through the bright shining moon.
God created a miracle,
On the third day of June.

I know times been rough,
And very hard.
If I had a little money,
I would of bought you a card.

But instead I took my thoughts,
And wrote them all down.
I hope there's a smile,
Beneath your quite, low frown.

You raised me when I was little,
And still will while I'm a man.
But life is short,
So have fun while you can.

I love you now,
And always will til I die.
But when your day comes,
That's the day I will cry.

So enjoy it while you can,
On this 34th year.
And alway's remember,
That I still love you and care.

Delvin E. Peeks

Written by Delvin to me on my 34th birthday.

Dear Justin,

My middle child for sure! As I look back on your growing up, you were, and still are, Justin! You had a rough job being born between Delvin and Jasmin, but you managed to come through as your own unique self. When you attended middle school, your principal called me one morning and of course I thought you had done something wrong. To the contrary, she was calling to simply tell me what a pure delight you were to have in her school. She said every day you would do something funny to just brighten up her day and she wanted to tell me how much she enjoyed you. *Who, Justin, my Justin? Of course, you didn't show this other side of his personality at home!*

I remember when I was trying to figure out what high school to send you to. It became very clear to me not to send you where your brother went because you needed to have your own space. I can't recall you ever getting suspended from school or being in a fight or doing any of the thousand crazy things a teenager can do. You were just chilling.

If you had a game system and a control in your hand, you were fine. I look back now and realize how blessed I was. I recall the time I showed up at your school when you indicated your grades were bad because the teachers didn't like you. Well, I came to Brashear High School to see for myself, and I stayed all day and went to all your classes. You were so out done. You didn't even sit with me in the cafeteria at lunch. No matter. It was the one and only time I had to make that trip. So, you grew up and you are your unique self.

I learned your language and I figured out that you don't say what you meant directly. It was more indirect and figurative. You're still a funny guy.

What makes me the proudest of you is also how you've grown into the man you are. The husband and father you are and are still becoming. I was tickled pink when you started working in the school system—not just any school but the same school you and I attended as children, and now you're there as faculty. When I hear children call you Mr. Peeks, my heart leaps.

You always had a great work ethic. I never had to worry about you not wanting to work and especially once you had a family. I see that old-school ethic in you that a man had to work and be a provider and a protector for his family.

I remember when you were in high school and you worked at Mitchell's Fish Restaurant. It was about midnight or so when you called me and woke me up from a dead sleep. You were so upset that you were still at work where your supervisor was asking you to do some menial task and you felt unfairly treated. With curlers still in my hair, I got in my car and came and got you, and of course I gave your supervisor a piece of my mind! That was another trip I only had to make once. You also never asked for a lot. Of a truth, if you had a game, you were good. You still today have a control stick of some kind in your hand. Some things don't ever change.

I'm watching you now also growing in your spirituality. I was super-elated when you and Alex and the kids all joined New Life. I always wanted you planted in a good church, but I was blessed you chose my church. You came in and right away tried to take over, as PK's do, but you are certainly a blessing in the house. I'm fully persuaded that God has a great plan for you and that you shall accomplish it. I'm proud also to be your mother, and to be your pastor.

Love you forever,
Mommy

❖ ❖ ❖ ❖

Dear Jasmin,

Loopy, my baby girl, my one and only daughter. I feel like this letter could be a whole book. First, I want to say, "I'm sorry." I feel like when I was so excited to finally have my daughter and I wanted to be best girlfriends; you were on a whole different page. You didn't want all the hugs, kisses, and fluffy stuff. Later, when you seemed to need it, I was on to the next thing. I never meant for you to feel like I mothered others and neglected you. You were always my little princess. When I heard the hurt, I imparted on you with my harsh words, it also was never my heart's desire for you to feel less then amazing.

As women now, I think we have finally landed on the same page. I truly feel we have a mutual respect and love for one another. Once you became a mother yourself, I think you may have understood mothering better. As I look back, you were always my little girl. When I was pregnant with you, the Peeks family was being flooded with boy babies. I'll never forget when you were born, and your dad called to tell his parents, I could hear your granddad scream all the way through the phone. He was elated! A girl, finally! When they came to see you, he brought long-stem American Beauty Roses.

I think when we have children that are just like us, it takes time to work out the clash. You have been a mini-me before there was a mini-me. Just as I've indicated with your brothers, I didn't have too hard of a time raising you. Unless, of course, you consider the time I had to come and sit in the class with you. Ms. Blango was the toughest teacher in Burgwin Elementary School, and you gave her a fit. Come to think of it, you gave every teacher a fit. Also, there was the time in middle school when you took my strip tickets to class and passed them out to your friends so you all could win in the snack drawings in your class. Now that I think about it, you were a tad bit more of a challenge than your brothers.

Good thing for both of us, God is able. He certainly turned our lives around. I love watching you blossom as a woman of God. I'm peacock proud when you minister and worship in the Lord. I'm sure you know that there isn't anything I wouldn't do for you, and I have always been grateful to have my Princess Jasmin.

If there was probably one thing I would change, it would be that when I prayed and asked God to give you a child that was just like you (payback), I would add, except when she's with her Nana (lol). I would say that strong women certainly do run in our family, and being one and birthing one, I wouldn't have it any other way. Jasmin Rae (Peeks) Harvey, as long as you live, I live. Love you much!

Always have, always will,
Mommy

To My wonderful children, Delvin, Justin and Jasmin,

I looked for a beautiful Maya-Angelou type poem that could express my sentiment, but after scrolling through numerous ones, I decided to write my own expression. I find myself filling up with emotion when I look back on how far you have come and how amazing you have grown up to be.

You are now all parents yourselves and I think you know how trial and error parenting is. We don't know all the right ways to do things to help our children, so we pray and do the best we can, and that's what I did. But you are all adults now with educations, jobs, spouses, children, a name for yourselves, and a good reputation! These are all that you can be proud of and, most of all, you all know who God is and have a relationship with Him.

I am a sentimentalist, and I've dreamed of having my own Hallmark movie called *Family Christmas* where all my family would spend a Christmas day together. Today, you have given me my dream. I know this holiday together took a great deal of sacrifice, but most times, things we really want will cost above and beyond—and this certainly did. That adds to my deep appreciation because I know you had to really push to be here—but we did it! I have had the distinct pleasure of being able to baptize both Justin and Jasmin and to officiate over all three wedding ceremonies of my children. You have no idea how very happy that made me, and all three of them have college degrees and wonderful spouses. Hallelujah! #soproudtobeyourmother

I am as proud of you as any mother could be of her children! You have done so many things that I am proud of and having my wonderful grandchildren is the cherry on top! I'm living the blessed life, and the men and woman that you are is a huge part of my joy! I'm godly proud to be your mother. So, with all the love my heart can hold, I love you three amazing, gifted, funny, thoughtful, and loving children, my children—Delvin, Justin, and Jasmin.

Christmas Fabulous 2016

I'm Nana

I THINK I did a pretty good job raising my three children; Delvin, Justin, and Jasmin, and I don't think they would disagree with that. We did all the things families were supposed to do. I used to say to my children that they would never be able to go on television and accuse me of being the bad mother. Not a chance! I loved being a mother and I am deeply proud, even today, of the amazing, wonderful children with whom God has blessed me.

Now having said that, I think I am a wonderful Nana. I have a sweatshirt that says, "If I knew how wonderful my grandchildren would be, I would have had them first." At the time of this writing, I have eight grandchildren, four boys (Dalen (1.2.2001), Marquis (10.30.2003), Austin (10.3.2010), and Liam (7.10.2014), and four girls (Leah 93.2.2014), Royal (9.7.2016), Graysen (11.2.2017), and Harmony (3.13.2018),and King (June11,2019) from my children and we have three more girls (Nia, Camille and Jasmine) on David's family side. Three of my granddaughters are currently two years old, and under. They are chilled out right now, except Royal, the two-year old. She's ready to go.

My first grandchild born was Dalen Ericson Peeks. He is the son of my firstborn, Delvin Ericson Peeks. You probably already know that, so let me share something you may not know. I will always remember the day Dalen was born. He was born in Cleveland Ohio, where his mother, Jenel Ross, lived. I was so excited about becoming a Nana, because up until this time my only grandchild was an iguana. His name was Iggy and he was Delvin's pet from high school all through college. I had no other grands, but Iggy didn't last forever and almost immediately after he departed this life, along came Dalen.

If you know anything about Cleveland, you know it's a snow-belt haven. I was working at Highmark at the time and so, when I got the call, I was elated. I called David aka Pappy and informed me that as soon as I got off work, we were headed to Cleveland. We loaded up the car with my mother, Jasmin, Justin, David, and I and off we went. Did I mention it was January? Yes, you got it; there was a snow blizzard and whiteout the entire trip. We couldn't even see the white dashes on the highway. Everyone was stressed, but me. I simply said, "Drive slowly, but keep driving." The trip from Pittsburgh to Ohio is a four-hour trip. This night it took about six hours.

Due to the extended driving time, when we arrived at the hospital well after nine o'clock, the visiting hours were over—but not for Nana! They graciously allowed us to go and visit with Jenel and my perfect new grandson. All I needed to do that day was to see his face and let him see mine. I wanted him to know he had a Nana who loved him very, very much. After we spent about an hour visiting and kissing and praying over our new baby, I turned to David and said, "Ok, it's time we get back on the road." Dalen's other grandmother; Ms. Vickie said," I know you're kidding." It had snowed the entire time we were there. I laughed but told them I was serious for I had to go to work the next day. Thank God that on the return trip, we were blessed to get behind a snowplow, and all the way back to Pittsburgh we had a plow escort.

Over the years, I made numerous trips up the highway to meet Jenel at McDonald's in Youngstown, Ohio and get my firstborn grandson and bring him back to Pittsburgh to be with his Nana and company. This year (2018-2019), Dalen is a senior in high school. He attends St. Mary–St Agnes in Ohio. In May, we anticipate attending his graduation and just the thought of it, tears (crying) me up.

I remember when Dalen got blessed in the Ross family church and of course we were all there. Ms. Vickie gave a wonderful celebration at her home afterwards and it was beautiful. I remember the little speech she gave in that house filled with family and friends. She said through the tears that streamed down her face, "I just pray that Dalen will always know the love that is in this room for him today; that he will always feel this degree of love." I agree. I love all my grandchildren, of course I do! And each of them is different and special in their own way, but that first one, it just must be special.

As God would have it, my other Nana memorable moment comes from Delvin's family. The birth of his daughter, Leah, was one for the books. The entire family was so excited when Delvin and Brandi got pregnant. They had some struggles with conception, but that was behind them and Brandi and Delvin were expecting. As I recall, Justin and Alex were also pregnant, and they were due about two or three days apart from one another. What a wonderful surprise for me. The due dates were around mid-July and that meant I would have two more grandbabies almost like twins.

I was in Orlando, Florida at a Bishop T.D. Jakes leadership conference (3.8.2014) when I got the call from Delvin that Brandi was in the hospital, and there were some medical problems with the pregnancy. First thing I did was start praying. Life has a way of reminding us sometimes just how helpless we are for things we can't control, and it was clear that medical situation was going to be one of those situations. So, the rough road began, and we did what we knew to do—pray. Each day we waited and prayed that Brandi would be able to hold the baby, because the longer she was in the womb, the better her chances would be for survival. In our family, we had hundreds of babies, but we found ourselves now in a strange place that we had never been before.

I remember the night like it was yesterday. I was getting dressed to go preach at New Jerusalem Holiness Church for the Women of Purpose Conference. I had preached at this conference for many, many years. I know the pastor, Reverend Amelia Jones, and her congregation very well, and they are like family. I had just pulled on my panty hose when my phone rang, and it was Delvin. When your son who is usually strong as a battle ax calls you and is crying, your heart just stops. Brandi had gone into labor and there was nothing they could do to stop it, and so we didn't know if the baby would survive. Brandi was only 23 weeks pregnant. I felt all my insides just drop and then I fell back on my bed. *Oh my goodness, what am I supposed to do?* I cried, "Dear God, please help my granddaughter and my family."

I tried to stay strong to encourage Delvin, but I was very concerned and sorely afraid for my unborn granddaughter. *How can I go and preach? How can I even concentrate? My heart is aching.* Then it happened, the deep thing we all need to happen when we feel ourselves losing it. The Holy Spirit rose up within me. He told me to call the church and tell them I had a family emergency, but I was on my way now.

When I arrived, the pastor and several others immediately greeted me and asked, "Are you okay"? I answered, "No. I'm not, but I will be. Give me a few minutes to just pray in the office and I'll be right out to preach." That's what they did, and that's what I did. I've had two occasions in my life where I knew very clearly as a preacher, if you can't preach God in a storm, you don't have the right to claim Him in the sunshine! So, I preached the God that I know, and trust can do anything but fail or lie. I preached Jesus! I preached out of a place that we don't too often have to go, but you better have it when you need it. I had told Delvin that I would be in service so when he would call me to leave me a message because I wouldn't be able to answer the phone.

As I was leaving the service, many people stopped me to express love and support, but I just wanted to run, get to my car, and listen to my messages. The last person to stop me was one of the church mothers, Mother Smith. She was in her nineties, and she wanted to tell me how much she loved me, and that she only came out that late at night to hear me preach. I hugged her and kissed her as I made my way to my car.

When I got to the car, I saw I had a voice message from Delvin, and as soon as I pushed the button to play it, there was a vigorous knocking on my car window. The same mother I had just hugged had fallen in the parking lot and hit her head and was bleeding. They asked me to please come out and pray for her while they waited for the ambulance to arrive. I dropped my phone and went and sat on the ground with her in my arms praying that God would keep her. By the time I got back to my phone again, I was almost numb. When I heard the first words out of Delvin's mouth, I wept with gratitude and thanksgiving. The baby was alive! Leah Michelle Peeks was born at 6:20 p.m., weighing one pound, eight ounces. She was certainly not out of the woods, but she was alive.

Our Leah, you are our miracle baby from God. You fought your way into this world, and you have leaped over every hurdle life threw at you. The long list of medical issues you had to overcome would take up a whole chapter, but you did it. Your father, mother, families, all the church families, and friends prayed vigorously for you. God answers prayer.

I love all my grandchildren, so I want to share something about all of you. No matter what your parents named you, Nana often had a nickname. Dalen was Butterball, Leah was Michelle, Austin was Nuppy, Liam was Gerber, Royal was Button, Graysen was Finally, and Harmony was Harmonica. I also want to say that I have grandchildren I never got to see or hold or kiss. I love them as well. I will see them when I get to heaven. I don't know why my most dramatic stories both came from Delvin's children, but each one is special, and I have a Nana story from each one of you.

Marquis is my genius child. He has been the brains from the beginning. He loves to read, and he retains what he reads. Then of course as a kid, he was always trying to correct me. I remember I had to tell him in my "I Mean it "voice, "If you say *actually* to me one more time . . ." Though he tried, but that's not happening. I certainly had to pull out the Nana rule book and tell him no matter how smart he is, I'm still smarter. He's the kind of person you expect to do very well in his career choice, and if you need a job, he'll probably be the one able to hire you.

Austin, you were my sidecar kid. When you were a baby and your family lived nearby, I could get my hands on you all the time, and I did. We would do the museums; libraries; Schenley Park playground (you loved the castle sliding board); road trips; train rides; and McDonald's kids' playroom. You were also one of the funniest kids I've ever known. You both said and did the funniest things. I told your dad he really missed an opportunity to make a kid's story book called *Austin*. Time gets away from us so fast and just like now, I can't even remember the things you did. I wish your dad had written the book.

My Liam! Oh my, were you a handful. I took you to the stores with me when you were about two years old. You brought a little action figure with you, as kids often do. When we left the store, we couldn't find your toy. I took you back to the car that was parked in a large mall parking lot. I opened the car door to see if you had left it in the car, and you took off! You ran across the parking lot like a loose cannon. You were fast, and I was old, so I couldn't catch you. I screamed for you to stop, and the more I screamed the faster you ran. All I could think was if a car would come, it wouldn't have seen you because you were just a little guy. *Please, God, help me!*

I finally was able to lunge after you and grab your jacket hood to stop you. I was so scared and out of breath, but I found the strength to whoop your butt. You had on blue jeans and you were still in pampers so it hurt me more then it hurt you. To make matters worse a stranger, who saw me whip you, got out of her car and told me, "That's enough of that!" I, in turn told her, "You better find your business and get in it and get outta mine!" There was another woman who saw the whole thing and she did try to comfort me. I took you into the grocery store, but I was so upset I couldn't even concentrate on what I went in there for. I called your father and told him, through my tears, that I was never watching you again, ever!

Your mom and dad knew how upset I was, and they said they understood. Apparently, I wasn't the only person you would take off running from. Surprisingly, you took a turn again and turned into the sweetest, kissy, lovey kid. So of course, I watched you a thousand times after that, but that day you sure got the best of me. None of the grands to that point had ever taken off running like that. Yes, you were a handful.

Greyson and Harmony, you girls are just little babies now. Greyson is the chunkiest, cutest baby in the world, and Harmony is the screamer. Greyson, you by far are the healthiest grandbaby. I'm using the word healthy to mean your thighs; you win the big leg contest hands down. I like to think that Harmony is just cutting teeth. Harmony is the cutie pie baby, and already I see signs of a strong personality. I don't have any stories yet on the two of you, because you're just beautiful, perfect babies. Before this writing is completed, my ninth grandchild should be born. He is due to arrive in June of this year (2019), and we're excited about his impending arrival and he will be the tie breaker. King Jaron Harvey was born on June 11, 2019 weighing seven pounds and six ounces and nineteen and a half inches long. At this time, I have no King story because the ink is still wet on you. However, I was holding you on my front porch I felt in my spirit that you will have a ministry of some sort, God-given and powerful. It made my heart smile again. Now, there is five boys and four girls and only God knows if there will be any more fruit on the tree...I think it would have to be an Act of God.

I really am very blessed to have the grandchildren I have. Nana loves all of you and I celebrate all the different personalities and strengths you have. I'm still certain that you will grow up to be amazing adults who I will be so proud of. As I hold you and kiss on you and tickle you as babies, I'm aware that there are some very gifted, intelligent, anointed, and blessed men and women growing inside of you. These little stories I've shared about you, to you, are probably times you don't even recall.

Of course not. These stories were my memories; they remind me of how fast time goes. I tried to hold on to a little piece of the past with each of you to make me smile on the inside. I also love taking pictures, as you will see, but that is truly the only way to make time stop. I have thousands and thousands of pictures of you all. When they put the capacity in our cellular phones to take pictures and make videos, it was game on for me. Being your Nana is my delight. You all make my heart *happy:* "A merry heart doeth good like a medicine: but a broken spirit drieth the bones" (Proverbs 17:22 KJV)

Dalen, Austin, Liam & Quis (12.2018)

Royal, Harmony, Nana, Greysen & Leah (12.2018)

My Journey to the Motherland

EARLIER IN THIS writing, I indicated that I had a great admiration for the African culture when it came to the ways that they would prepare their young for the real world. The term, rite of passage, is what I believe this culture lacks. At the time I wrote that statement, I also confessed that my perspective was one from a distance, I had never been to Africa. Well, as God would have it, that is no longer true. In the fall of 2018, I received an invitation from Dr. John Stanko, a local pastor and missionary, to accompany his group to Nairobi, Kenya, and I accepted. It was not a trip that was high on my bucket list but, I agreed ro fo because I knew without any doubt, that it was God. I've learned in my life that when God opens the door, our response is to walk therein.

We traveled from February 14 to 24, 2019. Traveling to Africa is not to be considered like taking a vacation. I would go so far as to say you don't just go to Africa; you encounter Africa. Dr. Stanko is the founder of a ministry, PurposeQuest, a non-profit that is committed to taking the help and hope of God and Christianity to the people and the places where it is needed. He has been going to Kenya for at least fifteen years now. In this time, he has opened an orphanage, a library, and a school, and has also partnered with numerous Kenyan preachers and businesspersons. He has done extensive training and counseling to help them discover their own purpose, and to begin to pursue their destiny.

One of my initial observations was that we consider Africa to be a Third World continent for a number of reasons, but when it comes to their faith and commitment to God, they make the United States look more like the lost continent. On Sunday when we attended a partner church, Harvest Fellowship Centre, we were invited after the first service to join one of the kids' Sunday School classes. They average several hundred children in their churches. In fact, later in our time, we went to visit another pastor who built a new church, and he housed six hundred children in their Sunday school. This is not near what is going on in our local assemblies.

A large part of our missionary trip was to engage the children, whether they were in school or an orphanage. There was something about the kids that was just hard to measure. They don't seem to be aware that they are poor. That's not their perception; it's ours. There is an intentional and deliberate directive to get the children all the education and knowledge they can possibly obtain. The goal is to turn the tide, with the future generations being the drivers in technology, politics, agriculture, education, and everything that makes progression progress. The Africans invest in their children. In this country, we have offered our children up as a sacrifice to the gods of this world. This is not an absolute, and it's certainly not the case for every family, but the people in high places and those with power is where we have failed.

When you see the children, who are living with minimal material possessions with the same childlike joy and laughter our children have, it makes you question our values. The focus on the children in Africa is to get the education to make a difference in their lives and the lives of the people around them. They can't afford to have the selfish mentality that we see all too often. Likewise, there are mannerisms with these children that American children lack. Integrity is a commodity that will always be worth its weight in gold. This is something I value and desire desperately for my descendants. Too many people have talents and gifts and even power, but lack integrity. When that's missing, it has the potential to bring it all down like a house of cards.

I'm convinced that many of my descendants will be very gifted, anointed, and talented—that's not what I'm concerned about. My concern is that those God-given abilities will be combined with respect, good morals, and integrity. My visit to Africa invigorated my drive to do what I can to prepare and equip my future generations with the characteristics that really matter. I realize that I will never forget the faces of some of the Kenyan children that I prayed on, hugged, and encouraged. I'll forever pray that they make it all the way to the top of their mountain journey. Every child born has a right to the best possible life available. As adults, we should do everything in our power to help them achieve that. My desire is to do my part, not just for mine, but for all those I can affect.

I decided before I returned home that I needed an answer for the question I knew I would get: "How was it?" I searched until I found a one-word answer: *impactful.* After I returned home, it took me several days to unpack my suitcase, and I felt like it took me longer to also unpack my experience. Everyday I'm still listening for "What else Lord?" I can say at this time; I believe I'll be returning to Africa again—and maybe even again.

Nana's Preaching

THESE FOLLOWING PAGES are a few sermons that I preached in my years as a pastor. I always had a passion for the family and what God had in mind when He created it. I did numerous messages to speak to that truth. Little boys will grow up and become men. Little girls will grow into women. There are many things they must be taught while they are young because it can happen faster than they think, and life won't wait for anyone to catch up.

God created the family and it consists of a man (husband) and a woman (wife) and prayerfully children—but not always. This is God's order and anything outside of this is out of order. The world has tried to redefine marriage and there is no end to what they will say is a legal marriage, but marriage was ordained By God and His plan for it has never changed.

"Faith in Family Matters"

Eulogy for Mrs Wilma Jeffries

Then Jesus went out from there and departed to the region of Tyre and Sidon. And behold, a woman of Canaan came from that region and cried out to Him, saying, "Have mercy on me, O Lord, Son of David! My daughter is severely demon-possessed."

But He answered her not a word.

And His disciples came and urged Him, saying, "Send her away, for she cries out after us."

But He answered and said, "I was not sent except to the lost sheep of the house of Israel."

Then she came and worshiped Him, saying, "Lord, help me!"

But He answered and said, "It is not good to take the children's bread and throw it to the little dogs."

And she said, "Yes, Lord, yet even the little dogs eat the crumbs which fall from their masters' table."

Then Jesus answered and said to her, "O woman, great is your faith! Let it be to you as you desire." And her daughter was healed from that very hour (Matthew 15:21-28)

Death is most times in our lives a very unwelcome guest, but we are always aware of his impending arrival. We have all known that someday we must leave this life and travel into the next, but it has most times still been very disturbing and annoying when it comes time.

Though we see death in a negative light, it does bring with its arrival a twofold blessing. On one hand, we think of the one who has departed and all the numerous occasions and conversations we shared with them (good and bad); then one the other hand, death causes us again to look into the mirror of our own life and assess what we see looking back at us. In this place, we often think of our own date with the door of transition and ask ourselves, *Am I prepared for my own death?* There is certainly a value to self-examination. It gives us a chance to look at our life and chose if we are pleased with what we see. The only problem is too often we don't see ourselves in the same way that others see us.

As believers, our advantage is the Holy Spirit inside of us who is there to illuminate and reveal to us the us in us. It's in this that the saying is magnified that sometimes the truth hurts, but it's the truth, nevertheless. In our reflection, we can also see if in fact our life has in any real significant way been an asset or a blessing to someone else's life. The song writer penned it in the lyrics "Is my living in vain? ".

In our text, we see a biblical account where faith has intervened in the matters in a family. The story opens with Jesus coming to Tyre and Sidon (a place where Gentiles were the majority of the population, not being godly people). It shows us that the Lord will deliberately come looking for people in the most unlikely places.

When this unlikely woman came to where Jesus was, she cried out to Him "Have mercy on me, O Lord, Son of David! My daughter is severely demon-possessed." This one plea is power packed with position, possession, and petition. First, it is *position*, because she cried out to Him. She probably fell at His feet and bowed down as was the custom when someone spoke to a person of high regard.

Then it is *possession*, because she knew Him. She called Him Lord and God and the One who could by mercy help her. And then *petition*, which was a divine intervention for her daughter, not for herself. She positioned herself to come to the Lord by her demonstration of faith, and because someone she no doubt loved very much needed deliverance. She had enough faith from even outside the house to believe that God could deliver her child. As the encounter continued it appears not to be going the way the mother might have thought it would.

> But He answered her not a word. And His disciples came and urged Him, saying, "Send her away, for she cries out after us." But He answered and said, "I was not sent except to the lost sheep of the house of Israel." Then she came and worshiped Him, saying, "Lord, help me!" (Matthew 15:22-24)

Jesus appears to ignore her, while the disciples or church folk wanted her put out. If that wasn't bad enough, Jesus disqualified her because of her nationality, which was not in her control. What was her response to all that? Her response to all this was to worship!

> Then she came and worshiped Him, saying, "Lord, help me!" (Matthew 15:25)

Her faith was again demonstrated in her determination not to be denied. You must know that oftentimes when you come for divine intervention, you must be committed to the task. It will not be a walk in the park, so remember, you must have faith to believe that God is able.

Finally, she had one more obstacle to overcome. This obstacle will surely separate the weak from the strong, and the faithful from the frail.

> But He answered and said, "It is not good to take the children's bread and throw it to the little dogs" (Matthew 15:26)

This text has forever been a hard pill for many to swallow. Did the Lord God call this desperate mother a dog?

> And she said, "Yes, Lord, yet even the little dogs eat the crumbs which fall from their masters' table" (Matthew 15:27)

The context of the text was that Jesus was proclaiming that He came for the house of Israel and to give this divine act to any other would be like taking the children's food and feeding it to their small pets. This final straw could have broken her but remember, she's not there for herself. It's her daughter, the daughter who is nowhere to be found—the daughter who we have no idea the things that she has done while she was sorely possessed—is not in the picture. It was her daughter and put yourself in her place with your own need: He's your son; she's your sister. We need the faith to stand on behalf of our family members who are not standing for themselves.

Is there anyone here today that is willing to muster up enough faith to make a difference in somebody else's life? Can you get past the past long enough to move with position, possession, and petition for someone even in your own family? And let this next verse provide the motivation to do it;

> Then Jesus answered and said to her, "O woman, great is your faith! Let it be to you as you desire." And her daughter was healed from that very hour (Matthew 15:28)

"A Tale of Two Mothers"

Now two women who were harlots came to the king and stood before him. And one woman said, "O my lord, this woman and I dwell in the same house; and I gave birth while she was in the house. Then it happened, the third day after I had given birth, that this woman also gave birth. And we were together; no one was with us in the house, except the two of us in the house. And this woman's son died in the night, because she lay on him. So, she arose in the middle of the night and took my son from my side, while your maidservant slept, and laid him in her bosom, and laid her dead child in my bosom. And when I rose in the morning to nurse my son, there he was, dead. But when I had examined him in the morning, indeed, he was not my son whom I had borne."

Then the other woman said, "No! But the living one is my son, and the dead one is your son."

And the first woman said, "No! But the dead one is your son, and the living one is my son."

Thus they spoke before the king.

And the king said, "The one says, 'This is my son, who lives, and your son is the dead one'; and the other says, 'No! But your son is the dead one, and my son is the living one.'" Then the king said, "Bring me a sword." So they brought a sword before the king. And the king said, "Divide the living child in two, and give half to one, and half to the other."

Then the woman whose son was living spoke to the king, for she yearned with compassion for her son; and she said, "O my lord, give her the living child, and by no means kill him!"

But the other said, "Let him be neither mine nor yours, but divide him."

So the king answered and said, "Give the first woman the living child, and by no means kill him; she is his mother."

And all Israel heard of the judgment which the king had rendered; and they feared the king, for they saw that the wisdom of God was in him to administer justice (1 Kings 3:16-28)

The biblical caption over this story in my Bible is "Solomon's Wise Judgment," and I can certainly see why. After all, remember it was Solomon's request when the Lord asked him what is it that he would desire from Him that God give him wisdom to rule over the people: Therefore give to Your servant an understanding heart to judge Your people, that I may discern between good and evil. For who is able to judge this great people of Yours?" (1 Kings 3:9). So in verse nine, Solomon asked for a heart to discern between good and evil, and by verse sixteen, he gets his first opportunity to do just that.

Today all over the world, people will be celebrating Mother's Day, and being myself a mother, I'm all for it. I would admonish all that can to in some way, shape, or form, extend a Happy Mother's Day to the mothers in their lives. I can certainly share also that for me, Mother's Day does not present a challenge because I have the sweetest Mother on God's green Earth. But I would be naïve if I thought that everyone had the same kind of mother I have. So, this biblical account clearly shows the tale of two mothers—two mothers who we would perceive were at polar opposite ends of the scale.

Today I want to look at this account and see what we don't see in the text. Sometimes the message is between the lines. The text explains that both women are harlots, living in the same house. The NKJV and the New American Standard translations both call the women harlots. The NIV calls them prostitutes and the Amplified refers to them as women pregnant outside of wedlock. Regardless of the translation, it is clear that these two women were dealing with obvious social and relational issues. There is no mention of any other family members, neither parents nor siblings, that might have been a part of their lives. Whether you consider this lifestyle against the backdrop of 500 BC or today, either way, it implies some serious social and personal challenges. This is a time when women were lower on the social scale, only a little more than an animal. Their only contribution was to bear children, a male child specifically.

For both of these women to make a choice to carry and deliver a child without the help of a male was a major decision. Also consider that with a child, it would no doubt impact their ability to continue in their lifestyle. Having a child is such a great responsibility and it adds so much more weight to your already heavy wagon, but they both had made that choice.

We know how their story goes that one delivered a male child one day, and three days later the other delivered a male child as well. If one had only been a girl, this would have ended their dilemma, but according to the text, no one was with them but each other. What that must have been like to deliver a child with no one but each other. Then the second mother laid upon her child and he died. What does it mean to have your son die? Desperation has its place at a time like this, and desperate times call for desperate measures. (is there anyone here today who under the right circumstance found yourself doing the wrong thing?) Sometimes it was the desperate things I survived that make me praise and shout to my Lord.

The Bible is loaded with stories of mothers who were *sheroes* (this is the female version of heroes). Eve, Sarah, Moses' mother, the widow who fed Elijah, Esther, Ruth, Naomi, and the woman whose daughter was sorely vexed with a demon, are just a few who come to mind. We know also in the Bible and in the real world that every woman who births a child is not a shero.

In life we all have an X, which is the place where our story began. It is the place that we started our journey. Only God knows all that we have endured along the way. Many have been abused, neglected, rejected, outcast, betrayed, and denied. Often, they had children on top of a mountain of pain and hurt, thinking that having a child might provide someone who might genuinely love them. And when a child is raised by a single mother, often the girls will go looking for that make-believe affirmation they yearn to feel—and the cycle continues.

Let me say by no means am I condoning women who have babies and don't do the necessary things to give their child a chance at a healthy, wholesome life. In fact, I stand very firmly against any such thing where the gift of children is being neglected or mistreated. I believe like the old mothers who would say, "They didn't ask to come here," so when they get here by their choices, then I stand in line with the mothers who sacrificed and denied themselves so they could provide for their children. Mothers who robbed Peter to pay Paul, who laid it away, who shopped night and day, who stood in lines and helped with algebra when they didn't understand it.

I stand with the women who did what it took! Good mothers, today we celebrate you. But today I want to also show some love to mothers who may have struggled with the call to be a mother. I want to show some agape love for you. I want to encourage you that there is a God who loves you and who can heal your hurts, mend your past, and deliver you from your bondage. It's not hard to love and celebrate lovable people, but God loved us all and we are not perfect people. I have enough faith to believe that a loving God can turn your life around. I ask what it must have felt like for the women whose son died. I have never had a son die, but I know God who loved us so much that He gave us His son to die so we could live.

We live in a diagnostic society where people are always diagnosing someone else's condition, but today I want to ask if there are any faith people in here who can testify that God can turn it around? The world is full of imperfect people who do what imperfect people do, but there is a light in the midst of our darkness and His name is Jesus. He's the God of a second chance.

So, before we judge so quickly the tale of two mothers, remember you might be one desperate time away from one desperate measure yourself. Today, I want to say to every mother: Find Jesus in your life.

Let the love that He has for you translate into the love you have for your children.

"We Speak Life to the King in You"

Do not rebuke an older man, but exhort *him* as a father, younger men as brothers, older women as mothers, younger women as sisters, with all purity (1 Timothy 5:1-2)

But as for you, speak the things which are proper for sound doctrine:[2] that the older men be sober, reverent, temperate, sound in faith, in love, in patience" (Titus 2:1)

Only a few weeks ago, we all celebrated Mother's Day and today we want to celebrate Father's Day. Technically, you can't have one without the other. With the way mankind is trying to play God, however, someday that might not be true, but today it is.

When God created mankind, we know He commanded them to be fruitful, multiply, and fill the earth. And the word the Bible uses in this context is they must *know their wife:*

- "Now Adam *knew* Eve *his wife,* and she conceived and bore Cain, and said, 'I have acquired a man from the LORD'"(Genesis 4:1)
- And Cain *knew his wife,* and she conceived and bore Enoch. And he built a city, and called the name of the city after the name of his son—Enoch" (Genesis 4:17)
- "And Adam *knew his wife* again, and she bore a son and named him Seth, 'For God has appointed another seed

for me instead of Abel, whom Cain killed'" (Genesis 4:25, emphasis added)

- Husbands, in the same way, live with your wives with an understanding of their weaker nature yet showing them honor as coheirs of the grace of life, so that your prayers will not be hindered" (1 Peter 3:7 HCSB)

When we read and study Scripture, we must do it from the perspective that God has a plan. He has a master plan for everything. In the book of beginnings, we clearly see God as the Master Builder or the sole supreme Creator of heaven and earth.

His desire is that the human race will fill the earthly realm with more humans so they can take care of this earth and worship God in relationship: ". . . having made known to us the mystery of His will, according to His good pleasure which He purposed in Himself" (Ephesians 1:9)

It was clear that relationship was also high on His priorities because He makes a statement after creating Adam that is was not good for man to be alone. Therefore, He pulled the woman out and gave her back to the man as complement and companion. This model of relationship was so important to God that He even uses it to model the relationship between mankind and the church:

> But as the church is subject to Christ, so also wives should be subject to their husbands in everything [respecting both their position as protector and their responsibility to God as head of the house] (Ephesians 5:24 AMP)

> However, each man among you [without exception] is to love his wife as his very own self [with behavior worthy of respect and esteem, always seeking the best for her with

an attitude of lovingkindness], and the wife [must see to it] that she respects and delights in her husband [that she notices him and prefers him and treats him with loving concern, treasuring him, honoring him, and holding him dear] (Ephesians 4:33 AMP)

Women, may I say this is where we struggle the most with our men. It would have been better if the text said we had to love him, honor him, and respect him, *if* he would behave in a way that we felt like he deserved it. Instead, the Bible instructs us in this way: "Wives, submit yourselves unto your own husbands, as unto the Lord" (Ephesians 5:22)

We know that the male struggle in our culture is a real struggle. Certainly, we know that they face some surreal challenges with jobs, education, social injustice, and numerous self-esteem problems. Because the model is broken (healthy homes) it's hard to learn how to imitate something that is distorted, and therefore, they mirror what they see.

John the disciple saw the Lord from the beginning, and he expressed that in his writing when he provided a peak at the blueprint God had for us:

He was in the beginning with God. ³ All things were made through Him, and without Him nothing was made that was made. In Him was life, and the life was the light of men (John 1:2-4)

John saw that Jesus who was with the Father and in Him was life, and the life was the light of men.

Light is knowledge or understanding, and *knowledge* is power— and power equips and enables. And enabled is purposed and purposed is lining up with the plan. And the plan is that we would have life and that more abundant. All men please stand. I have come today to speak life into you.

- You are made in God's image and He has a plan for you.
- You are a king.
- Rise up to your crown.
- You are loved.
- You are forgiven. Your past is behind you. Your future is waiting for you to arrive.
- You are strong.
- You are gifted.
- You have a purpose.
- You are intelligent.
- You have a king in you.
- Your sons need you and your daughters need you.
- Your wife needs you.
- Your community needs you.
- I speak life into you.
- Jesus loves you.
- The power of the Holy Spirit is upon you.
- You are made whole in Christ.
- You are the head. You are not the tail.
- You are respected. You are important. You are needed!
- There is a king in you!

"My Family, God's Family"

Adam made love to his wife, Eve, and she became pregnant and gave birth to Cain. She said, "With the help of the Lord, I have brought forth a man. Later

she gave birth to his brother Abel. And Abel kept the
flocks, and Cain worked the soil (Genesis 4:1-2)

This week a group of thirteen woman traveled to Dallas, Texas
for Bishop T. D. Jakes' (Thomas Dexter Jakes Sr.) WTAL (Woman,
Thou Art Loosed) Conference. I along with other New Life women
and woman from other churches from around the city also attended.
The conference was focused on women coming together from all
over the world and being exposed to women who have shattered the
glass ceiling in the business world and have defied all the odds against
them. The conference platform was an accumulation of billionaires,
CEO's, medical doctors, and preachers.

It was a combination of instruction and information to restore,
rebrand, rebuild, and believe that we all could, if we put our minds
to it, stretch out of the box. We had one lecture, workshop, and panel
discussion after another. To be honest, it was almost too much to even
be exposed to at one time. Every presenter, whether from the business
world or the church, was excellent in their presentations, and they were
thoroughly prepared and qualified to stand in the place where they stood.

We danced, we shouted, we laughed, and we cried. We got all
we went for and even more, but there was an underlying topic that,
though it was not on the agenda, was present at every session. There
was an uninvited guest at the table for every session. This guest could
not be and would not just go away. As I look back, I can say no one
confronted it head on, but it was knit somehow into every session and
every topic, whether from a corporate perspective or a biblical one,
it was always there.

Bishop T.D. Jakes and his wife, Serita, have five children:
Jermaine, Jamar, Cora, Sarah, and Thomas Jakes Jr. Both of their
daughters are preachers and entrepreneurs in their own right; of the
sons, not so much is known.

Bishop Jakes delivered the final message for the Master Class conference, and it was at the end of the message and after all the accolades, the cat finally got out of the bag. We must embrace the gift, the blessing, and the responsibility of family. By the moving of the Holy Spirit, Bishop Jakes called all his daughters, son-in-law, wife, and grandchildren to the stage.

With tears running down his face, he made a public vow to do all that he could to stand by his family, right or wrong, good or bad, and to always be there for them. He told his grandchildren that he may not be there to go the distance with them, but that he would do all he could to give them a strong start. There was a flood of emotion and love.

This week we celebrate family. I realized as I reflected back over the entire conference that family was always knit somehow someway into the picture of every story. Sometimes the family dynamic was positive, and then other times maybe not so much, but it was always present.

God created families and families do matter. As we read in our Scripture passage today, Genesis is the birthplace of the human family. The husband and the wife come together in love and multiply, and the children start coming—and from there we're off to the races. Family consists of children, sisters, brothers, aunts, uncles, cousins, grandchildren, and on and on and on.

Having a family is a gift from God; no other creation has the capacity to have family except humans. Your family is your first place of learning and shaping, of encouraging and challenging, and most of all, loving. Not that we agree with everything our family does, but we love them. It's a strange kind of thing that we can't always understand or explain. Maybe it the same thing that God says when He thinks of His love shown towards us.

There are things we do or don't do, and the driving force is because of our family, because we love them and want the best for them always. They have our DNA, our blood line and character, our resemblance. They are a mini version of us. Sometimes we're glad they do, and other times, we don't want them to do what we do.

Our first family is the one we were born into. We didn't pick our family, but God in His infinite wisdom gave us to them. And we know that everyone didn't get a good deal on the family they have, but the good news is there is another family available to us.

> That was the true Light which gives light to every man coming into the world. He was in the world, and the world was made through Him, and the world did not know Him. He came to His-own, and His-own did not receive Him. But as many as received Him, to them He gave the right to become children of God, to those who believe in His name: who were born, not of blood, nor of the will of the flesh, nor of the will of man, but of God (John 1:9-13)

God has also given us the amazing opportunity to be a part of the family of God. In this family, we are now the sons and daughters of God. He is the loving Father, who also has promised to protect us and provide for us. He is also the one we desire to imitate.

> He's the father to the fatherless.
> He's the mother to the motherless.

You can rest in the loving arms of God and listen for His heartbeat. He will provide for you. He will protect you. He will lead you in the right directions because He knows the way. Don't allow the hurt of any other relationships prevent you from feeling the agape love of God. You are part of my family; you are part of His family.

Where Do We Go from Here?

King Solomon was the wisest and the wealthiest man who ever lived. He was the beloved son of King David, and the Lord granted to him both wisdom and wealth that would never be exceeded. Imagine what your life would be like with these two treasures. He could possess anything he wanted, and he had more God-given divine knowledge than anyone else. If there ever was a person who I would want to sit down and talk to, he would be the one (after Jesus, of course). King Solomon is long since gone, but he left his writings to help us get answers to questions we might ask him. See what King Solomon says about life and living it.

The words of the Preacher, the son of David, king in Jerusalem. Vanity of vanities, saith the Preacher, vanity of vanities; all is vanity. What profit hath a man of all his labour which he taketh under the sun? One generation passeth away, and another generation cometh: but the earth abideth for ever (Ecclesiastes 1:1-4 KJV)

In other translations, he is referred to as the teacher. He was in fact both. He wrote the biblical books of Proverbs, Ecclesiastes, and Song of Solomon. In the book of Ecclesiastes, he writes what we call the sum of the whole matter, or the bottom line to life:

And so, we come to the end of this musing over life. My advice to you is to remember your Creator, God, while you are young: before life gets hard and the injustice of old age comes upon you—before the years arrive when pleasure feels far out of reach—before the sun and light and the moon and stars fade to darkness and before cloud-covered skies return after the rain. Remember Him before the arms and legs of the keeper of the house begin to tremble—before the strong grow uneasy and bent over with age—before toothless gums aren't able to chew food and eyes grow dim. Remember Him before the doors are shut in the streets and hearing fails and everyday sounds fade away—before the slightest sound of a bird's chirp awakens the sleeping but the song itself has fallen silent. People will be afraid of falling from heights and terrifying obstacles in the streets. Realize that hair turns white like the blossoms on the almond tree, one becomes slow and large like a gluttonous grasshopper, and even caper berries no longer stimulate desire. In the end, all must go to our eternal home while there are mourners in the streets. So before the silver cord is snapped and the golden bowl is shattered: before the earthen jar is smashed at the spring and the wheel at the well is broken—before the dust returns to the earth that gave it and the spirit-breath returns to God who breathed it, let us remember our Creator. Life is fleeting; it just slips through your fingers. All vanishes like mist.

So be warned, my child, of anything else that might be said! There is no end to writing books, and excessive study only exhausts the body. And, when all is said and done, here is the last word: worship in reverence the one True God, and keep His commands, for this is what God expects of every person. For God will judge every action—including everything done in secret—whether it be good or evil (Ecclesiastes 12:1-8, 12-14 Voice)

What is Nana saying? First, I want you to know that you were loved long before you were even born, not just by me, but also by God. He is real and He wants you to know that. If things had gone the way He wanted them to, I'd be able to sit down and tell you these things face to face. We would have all lived eternally with Him. Mankind disobeyed God's instruction, however, and now sin has come into the world and people will die. The good news (the gospel) is that God's love for us never stopped, and now we have another chance to love Him back and to spend eternal life with Him in heaven, which is also real.

I already know that I'll be in heaven with God when I die. My heart's desire and my prayer is that you will someday be there, too. I want you to live the blessed life possible. I want you to know what it feels like to be a child of God. I want you to live a life full of favor with God and man. I want you to be kind, compassionate, and caring. I want you to have provision and protection. I want you to find your purpose and fulfill it according to what God has in mind for you. I want you to be men and woman of integrity with a good reputation. I want you to be both wise and humble.

I want you to be a servant and not a master. I want your words to be life giving and not destructive. I want you to know that you are not perfect, but to not be satisfied with your imperfections. I want you to know you never have to settle for less than what God has for you. I want you to know you are not common. I want you to know that you must respect yourself by showing respect for others. I want you to know that you never have to use profanity (cuss). You will have good English that you can use. Always try to use positive words even to express a negative situation.

I want you to know you will make mistakes, but as long as you learn something constructive from them, they will be good for your character. I want you to know that some battles you will win by simply refusing to fight. You need to know there is always someone watching you and God sees and hears everything. I want you to always pray and talk to God and believe that He hears you and He will answer. I want you to know that sometimes the answer is no.

There is so much that I want you to know about who I am or who I was so it may help you in some way to know who you are and who God has created you to be. It was way too much to just put in an obituary.

I want you to know that times goes faster and faster the older you get, so you must live like you believe it. I want you to laugh more then you cry—but know that we all cry sometimes. I want you to know that your Nana, Great Nana, Great-Great Nana is loving you right now and will always be loving you. I want you to know that when you feel the gentle winds against your skin, or a cold snowflake on your cheek, or the warm sun against your face, that it's your Nana sending you a kiss.

Printed in the United States
By Bookmasters